D1272688

Jewelry

FIELD GUIDE

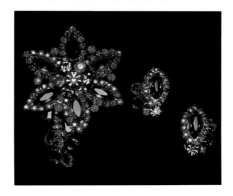

Leigh Leshner

Values and Identification

©2005 by KP Books

Published by

kp books
An Imprint of F+W Publications

700 East State Street • Iola, WI 54990-0001
715-445-2214 • 888-457-2873

Our toll-free number to place an order or obtain a free
catalog is (800) 258-0929.

Library of Congress Catalog Number: 2004099298

ISBN: 0-87349-982-4

Designed by: Wendy Wendt
Edited by: Mary Sieber

Printed in U.S.A.

Contents

Introduction

By Kyle Husfloen

Jewelry has held a special place for humankind since prehistoric times, both as an emblem of personal status and as a decorative adornment worn for its sheer beauty. This tradition continues today. We should keep in mind, however, that it was only with the growth of the industrial revolution that jewelry first became inexpensive enough so that even the person of modest means could own a piece or two.

Only since around the mid-19th century did certain forms of jewelry, especially pins and brooches, begin to appear on the general market as a mass-produced commodity, and the Victorians took to it immediately. Major production centers for the finest pieces of jewelry remained in Europe, especially Italy and England, but less expensive pieces were also exported to the booming American market, and soon some American manufacturers also joined in the trade.

Especially after the Civil War era, when silver and gold supplies grew tremendously in the United States, jewelry in silver or with silver, brass, or gold-filled (i.e., gold-plated) mounts began flooding the market here. By the turn of the 20th century, all the major mail-order companies and small town jewelry shops could offer a huge variety of inexpensive jewelry pieces aimed at not only the feminine buyer but also her male counterpart.

As with all types of collectibles, yesterday's trinket can become today's treasure, and so it is with jewelry. Today jewelry collecting ranks as one of the most popular areas of collecting, and with millions of pieces on the market, any collector—no matter what their budget—can find fascinating and attractive jewelry to collect. Of course the finest and rarest examples of antique or "pre-owned" estate jewelry can run into the many thousands of dollars, but thanks to the mass-production of jewelry over the last century and a half, there is lots for the less well-heeled to enjoy.

Inexpensive jewelry of the late 19th and early 20th centuries is still widely available and often at modest prices. Even more in demand today is what is called "costume jewelry," that is, well-designed jewelry produced of inexpensive materials and meant to carefully accent a lady's ensemble. The idea for costume jewelry was launched in the 1920s by the famous French clothing designer, Coco Chanel, and her inspiration immediately took root. From that time forward any woman of taste could afford well-designed and attractive pieces that mirrored the glitziest bijoux but were available at a fraction of the cost. Today costume jewelry of the 20th century has become one of the most active areas in the field of collecting, and some of the finest pieces, signed by noted designers and manufacturers, can reach price levels nearly equal to much earlier and scarcer pieces.

Whether you prefer the glittering and gaudy or the subtle and elegant, jewelry offers the collector a vast realm from which to choose. In addition to being an investment, the owner also has the opportunity to wear and share the beauty or whimsy of a piece of the past.

In preparing the listings in this book, we have done our best to provide detailed and accurate descriptions of the pieces included, but, as always, use the prices listed only as a guide. Jewelry prices, as in every other major collecting field, are influenced by a number of factors, including local demand, quality, condition, and rarity. As market prices have risen in recent years, it has become even more important for the collector to shop and buy with care. Learn as much as you can about your favorite area of jewelry, keep abreast of market trends, and stay alert to warnings about alterations, repairs, or reproductions that can be found in the market. Use this book as a reference and general guide to broaden your understanding and appreciation of the wonderful world of jewelry collecting, and it can serve you well.

Special thanks to jewelry expert Leigh Leshner, author of *Rhinestone Jewelry, A Price and Identification Guide*, *Costume Jewelry Identification and Price Guide*, *Vintage Jewelry, A Price and Identification Guide, 1920-1940s*, and *American Plastic Jewelry,* and collectibles expert Kyle Husfloen, editor of *Antique Trader Jewelry Price Guide* and the annual *Antique Trader Antiques & Collectibles Price Guide*.

American Painted Porcelain

BROOCHES

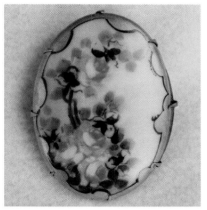

Belt buckle brooch, oval, decorated w/roses and
greenery on a polychrome ground, burnished gold scalloped
border outlined in black, gold-plated bezel, ca. 1900-1917,
1 15/16" x 2 11/16".. **$110**

Belt buckle brooch, oval, w/horse chestnut branch on baby blue ground, gold-plated bezel, ca. 1900-1917, 2" x 2 1/2"...**$150**

Belt buckle brooch, oval, decorated w/a white pansy, accented w/white enamel, on a burnished gold ground, gold-plated bezel, 1900-1917, 1 11/16" x 2 1/4"..........................$75

Belt buckle brooch, oval, decorated w/a profile of a woman wearing a pink top and white shawl, pink roses in her curly brown hair, black choker at her neck, burnished gold rim, gold-plated bezel, signed "M.e.M.," 1900-1917, 1 7/8" x 2 3/8"..**$175**

Belt buckle brooch, oval, decorated w/blue bachelor buttons and greenery on a polychrome ground, irregular burnished gold border outlined in black, gold-plate bezel, 1900-1917, 1 7/8" x 2 5/8"..**$95**

Belt buckle brooch, oval, decorated w/an art nouveau-
style water lily design outlined w/raised paste, petals filled in
w/lavender enamel, burnished green and gold background,
gold-plated bezel, 1900-1917, 1 7/8" x 2 5/8".
.... **$110**

Brooch, diamond-shaped, decorated w/a water lily and waterscape w/white enamel highlights, sky and clouds in background, burnished gold rim, gold-plated bezel, ca. 1930-1940s, 7/8" sq..**$35**

Brooch, heart-shaped, decorated w/a pink and a ruby rose w/leaves on a polychrome ground, white enamel accents, burnished gold rim, gold-plated bezel, 7/8" x 7/8".............**$30**

Brooch, long oval, decorated w/forget-me-nots and leaves
on a pastel polychrome ground, white enamel highlights,
burnished gold rim, gold-plated bezel, 1" x 1 3/4"............**$45**

Brooch, oval, decorated w/an art nouveau maiden's portrait surrounded by forget-me-nots on an ivory ground, white enamel highlights, framed by burnished gold raised paste scrolls and dots, gold-plated bezel, 1 1/4" x 1 5/8".............**$80**

Brooch, oval, decorated w/a large pink rose and green leaves on a light blue ground, burnished gold rim, gold-plated bezel, 1 1/8" x 1 3/8"..**$40**

Brooch, oval, decorated w/a tropical river landscape in polychrome colors, signed on the lower left "OC" (Olive Commons, Coconut Grove, Florida), gold-plated bezel, ca. 1920s, 1 3/8" x 1 1/4"..**$75**

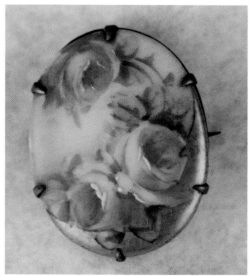

Brooch, oval, decorated w/pink roses and greenery on a
pastel polychrome ground, accented w/white enamel, edged w/
burnished gold on one side, gold-plated bezel, ca. 1890-1920,
1 1/16" x 1/3/8". **$45**

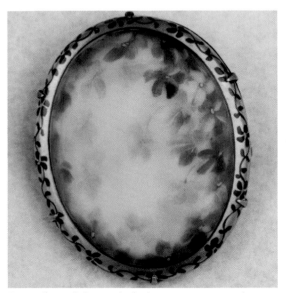

Brooch, oval, decorated w/violets on an ivory ground,
burnished gold border superimposed w/a black line border
design of violets and vines, ca. 1900-1915, 1 1/2" x 2" **$75**

Brooch, oval, decorated w/an art nouveau-style woman's bust, w/poppies in her hair, gold-plated bezel, 1900-1915, 1 1/2" w x 2". **$90**

Brooch, oval, decorated w/violets and leaves on a polychrome ground, framed by diagonals of burnished gold bordered w/ raised paste scrolls and dots, gold-plated box setting w/twisted rope border, ca. 1880-1920, 1 3/4" x 2 1/8". **$100**

Brooch, oval, decorated w/columbine and greenery on a polychrome ground, burnished gold rim, gold-plated bezel, ca. 1900-1920, 1 13/16" x 2 3/16"..**$75**

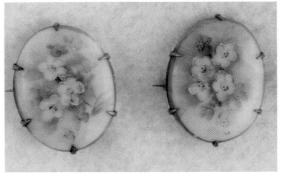

Brooches, oval, decorated w/forget-me-nots on a pale pink
and blue ground w/white enamel highlights on petal edges,
burnished gold rims, gold-plated bezels, gold wear, ca. 1900-
1920, 13/16" x 1", pr..**$70**

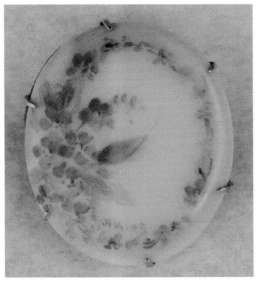

Brooch, oval, decorated w/forget-me-nots on a pale yellow center w/pale blue border, gold-plated bezel, signed "A. Jibbing," ca. 1900-1920, 1 3/8" x 1 1/2"..............................**$75**

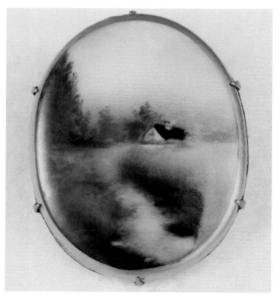

Brooch, oval, decorated w/a sunset landscape scene w/house by stream, trees in background, burnished gold rim, gold-plated bezel, 1 1/2" x 1 15/16". **$125**

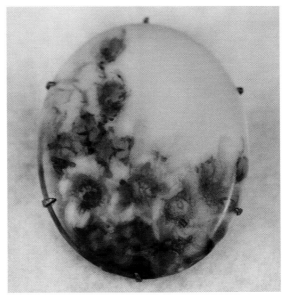

Brooch, oval, decorated w/pink wild roses and buds w/green leaves on an ivory ground, gold-plated bezel, ca. 1900-1920, 1 5/8" x 2 1/16"...**$65**

Brooch, oval, decorated w/a water lily on a watery blue green background, gold-plated bezel, ca. 1900-1920, 1 5/8" x 2 1/16"..**$50**

Brooch, oval, decorated w/a conventional-style lavender iris
and green leaves outlined in black on a yellow lustre ground
w/white enamel highlights on petal edges and yellow enamel
highlights on flower centers, burnished gold rim, gold-plated
bezel, ca. 1900-1920, 1 5/8" x 2 1/8"....................................**$75**

Brooch, oval, decorated w/a large red and purple pansy on a burnished gold ground, gold-plated bezel, 1 1/2" x 1 7/8".
.... **$75**

Brooch, oval, decorated w/pink and white and ruby roses and green leaves on a rich blue ground w/white enamel highlights, burnished gold border and rim, gold-plated bezel, ca. 1940s, 1 1/2" x 2"...**$65**

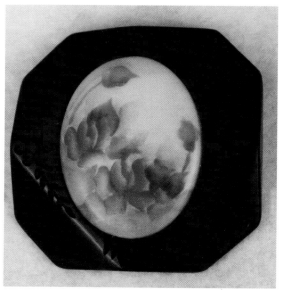

Brooch, porcelain medallion, oval, inset in black plastic, decorated w/ruby roses and greenery on an ivory ground, ca. 1910-1930, 1 3/8" x 1 3/4"..**$50**

Brooch, rectangular, decorated w/a tropical scene of palm tree in white on a platinum ground, painted by Olive Commons, Miami, Florida, sterling silver bezel, ca. 1920-1940s, 3/4" x 1"..**$80**

Brooches, round, decorated w/pink and ruby roses and
green leaves on a polychrome ground, burnished gold rim,
gold-plated bezel, 7 /8" d., pr. **$70**

Brooch, round, w/forget-me-nots and leaves, border of raised paste dots covered w/burnished gold, gold-plated bezel, ca. 1890-1910, 1 1/8" d. **$35**

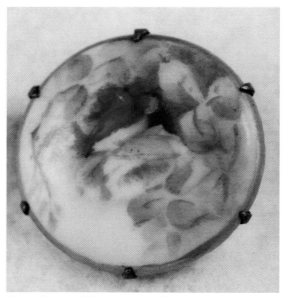

Brooch, round, decorated w/a pink and a ruby rose and
greenery on a pastel polychrome ground, burnished gold rim,
gold-plated bezel, ca. 1890-1910, 1 3/16" d. **$40**

Brooch, round, decorated w/a white pansy on a matte black ground, gold-plated bezel, ca. 1890-1910, 1 1/8" d. **$30**

Brooch/pendant, oval, decorated w/an elegant woman
wearing a pale blue shawl, accented w/turquoise jeweled
necklace, white enamel pearls in headband and on shawl,
bordered by raised paste scrolls and dots covered w/burnished
gold and accented by turquoise enamel jewels, polychrome
ground, set in gold-plated box setting w/twisted rope border,
ca. 1880-1920, 2 1/16" x 2 1/2". **$200**

MISCELLANEOUS PINS

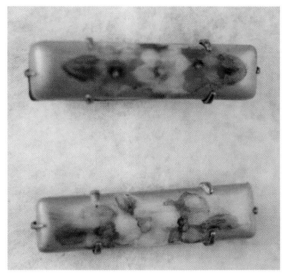

Cuff pins, rectangular, decorated w/forget-me-nots on a
   burnished gold ground, gold-plated bezel, ca. 1900-1915, 1/4"
   x 1 1/4", pr. **$45**

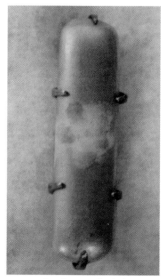

Cuff pin, rectangular, decorated w/a forget-me-nots on a burnished gold ground, gold-plated bezel, ca. 1900-1915, 1/4" x 1". **$12**

Flapper pin, oval, decorated w/a stylized, elegant red-haired woman wearing blue dress and fur stole, pink flower and large comb in her hair, white ground w/burnished gold border, gold-plated bezel, ca. 1922-1930, 1 11/16" x 2 1/8"..**$85**

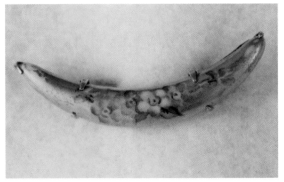

Handy pin, crescent-shaped, decorated w/forget-me-nots
and leaves on a burnished gold ground, gold-plated bezel, ca.
1890-1915, gold wear, 1 13/16"..**$30**

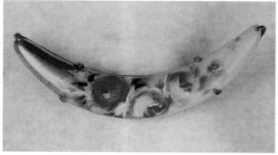

Handy pin, crescent-shaped, decorated w/pink and ruby roses and green leaves on an ivory ground, w/white enamel highlights and one burnished gold tip, gold-plated bezel, ca. 1890-1915, 2 3/16" w..**$45**

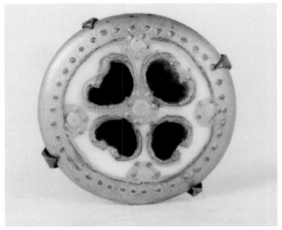

Hatpin, circular head, decorated w/a conventional geometric design in raised paste dots and scrolls, covered w/burnished gold, turquoise enamel jewels, cobalt blue flat enamel, gold-plated bezel, ca. 1905-1920, 1" d., 6 3/8" shaft.............. **$110**

Hatpin, circular head, decorated w/pink roses and greenery on a pale blue and yellow ground, burnished gold border, gold-plated bezel, ca. 1890-1920, some gold wear, 1" d., 7 3/4" shaft...**$115**

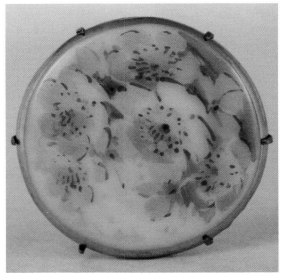

Hatpin, circular head, decorated w/wild pink and white
roses and greenery w/yellow enamel accents in flower centers,
burnished gold border, gold-plated bezel, ca. 1890-1915,
1 1/4" d., 9" shaft..**$185**

Hatpin, circular head, decorated w/ruby roses and green
leaves, embellished w/burnished gold scrolls, gold-plated bezel,
head 1 3/8" d., shaft 7 3/4" l. (ILLUS. of head)................**$125**

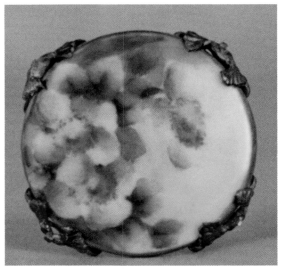

Hatpin, circular head, decorated w/pink wild roses and greenery on a yellow ground, burnished gold rim, gold-plated filigree setting, head 1 1/16" d., shaft 9" l.........................**$135**

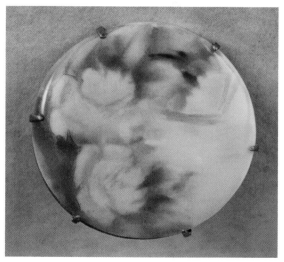

Hatpin, decorated w/yellow roses and leaves on a yellow, yellow brown, and brown background, gold-plated bezel, ca. 1890-1920, 1 1/4" d., 7 3/4" shaft.....................................**$115**

PENDANT

Pendant, oval, decorated w/forget-me-nots on a pastel
polychrome ground w/white enamel highlights and burnished
gold rim, gold-plated bezel, ca. 1900-1925, 1 1/4" x
1 3/4"...**$65**

SHIRTWAIST BUTTONS

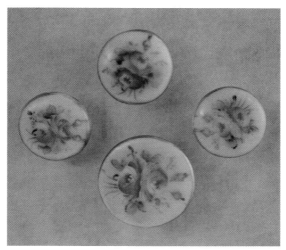

Shirtwaist buttons, round w/shanks, decorated w/pink
roses and greenery on a pastel polychrome ground, burnished
gold rims, ca. 1900-1920, gold wear, 5/8" d., one 7/8" d.,
the set. **$50**

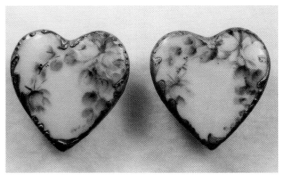

Shirtwaist buttons, heart-shaped, decorated w/pink
roses, raised paste scrolled border covered w/burnished gold,
ca. 1890-1910, 1 1/8" x 1 3/16", pr. **$75**

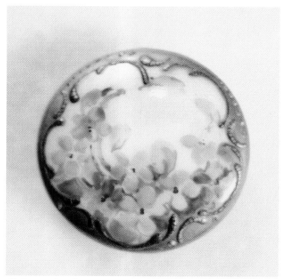

Shirtwaist button, round w/shank, decorated w/forget-me-nots, raised paste scrolled border covered w/burnished gold, signed "GHL," 1 1/26" d. **$30**

Shirtwaist button, round w/shank, decorated w/a girl's profile on multicolored ground, burnished gold rim, 1 7/16" d...**$75**

Shirtwaist button, round w/eye, decorated w/a
conventional stylized long blossom flanked by pointed oval
leaves in pale yellow, dark blue and black on a burnished gold
ground, 1 1/16" d..**$30**

Shirtwaist button, oval w/shank, decorated w/a three-leaf clover in green on a yellow and brown ground, burnished gold rim, 7/8" x 1 1/16". **$20**

Shirtwaist button, round w/shank, decorated w/the bust portrait of a young blonde-haired girl, wearing a pale blue dress, against a shaded yellow to black ground, 1 3/8" d.
....**$80**

Shirtwaist buttons, round, each decorated w/a
geometric pinwheel design in light blue, black and gold
trimmed w/burnished gold dots and a center turquoise
"jewel," on a burnished gold ground, two 1" d., three 7/8" d.,
the set. **$115**

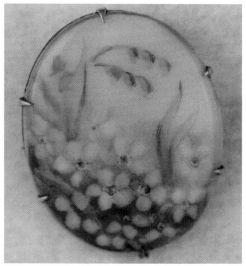

Shirtwaist set, oval brooch and two round buttons w/
shank; each decorated w/forget-me-nots and greenery on a
pastel polychrome ground, burnished gold rim, gold-plated
bezel, brooch 1 1/4" x 1 3/4", buttons 15/16" d., the set (ILLUS.
of brooch) **$90**

Shirtwaist set, oval cuff links and three round buttons w/ shanks; decorated w/clusters of violets on pale yellow ground, burnished gold rim, gold-plated bezel on cuff links, ca. 1900-1915, cuff links 3/4" x 1 1/4", buttons 1 1/4" d., the set.
.... **$175**

WATCH CHATELAINE

Watch chatelaine, oval, decorated w/a woman wearing a rose-colored bodice, light shading to dark warm green ground, set in gold-plated rim w/twisted gold edge, ca. 1880s, 1 1/8" x 1 3/8"..**$125**

Antique Jewelry

BRACELETS

Bracelet, bangle-type, citrine, diamond and enamel, hinged design centering a large, faceted, heart-shaped citrine surrounded by old mine- and rose-cut diamonds w/two triangular-shaped citrines on the sides, each decorated w/rose-cut diamonds set in trefoil designs, mounted in 14k yellow gold w/royal blue enameled background, 6 1/2". **$3,450**

Bracelet, bangle-type, 18k gold, Victorian Etruscan Revival-style, hinged knot design w/ball terminals, overall bead and wire twist decoration. **$2,415**

Bracelet, bangle-type, gold (14k yellow) and amethyst, hinged design centered by a prong-set rectangular-cut amethyst within an openwork foliate frame, dated 1908, Edwardian..**$690**

Bracelet, gold, bangle-type, 14k, hinged bangle w/four-leaf clover mount and seed pearl stem over an interlocking loop design, three green stone accents, Edwardian...............**$264**

Gold bracelet with emeralds and pearls, $5,573.

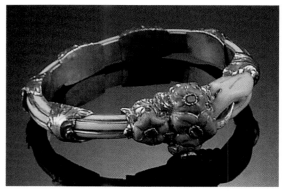

Gold and enamel hand bracelet, $2,300.

Bracelet, bangle-type, art nouveau-style pierced and chased foliate design in 14k yellow gold, 7 1/2".................. **$1,035**

Bracelet, bangle-type, diamond, enamel, platinum and gold, the tested 14k yellow gold mount set on the top portion w/a filigree platinum chase-work floral design set w/93 round old European- and rose-cut diamonds weighing about 1.75 carats within a cobalt blue guilloché enamel field, ca. 1910, Edwardian...**$2,760**

Bracelet, emerald, diamond and gold, articulated barrel-shaped links w/the 16 center link section set w/an emerald flanked by rose-cut diamonds, ca. 1880, Victorian, w/original box. **$2,875**

Bracelet, emerald, pearl and gold, 18k yellow gold bangle w/filigree gold work containing three emerald-cut emeralds, four pearls, surrounded by rose-cut diamonds and accented with eleven small round-cut emeralds, ca. 1890 (ILLUS. p. 63)... **$5,573**

Bracelet, enamel and 18k yellow gold, flexible gold and white enamel links w/foliate repoussé spacers completed by a hand clasping a basket of blue enamel flowers, surmounted by pink stones, French assay mark, chips and repair to enamel, Victorian (ILLUS. p. 64). **$2,300**

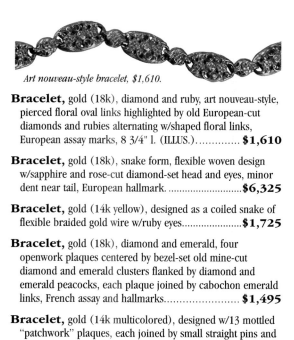

Art nouveau-style bracelet, $1,610.

Bracelet, gold (18k), diamond and ruby, art nouveau-style, pierced floral oval links highlighted by old European-cut diamonds and rubies alternating w/shaped floral links, European assay marks, 8 3/4" l. (ILLUS.).............. **$1,610**

Bracelet, gold (18k), snake form, flexible woven design w/sapphire and rose-cut diamond-set head and eyes, minor dent near tail, European hallmark. **$6,325**

Bracelet, gold (14k yellow), designed as a coiled snake of flexible braided gold wire w/ruby eyes.....................**$1,725**

Bracelet, gold (18k), diamond and emerald, four openwork plaques centered by bezel-set old mine-cut diamond and emerald clusters flanked by diamond and emerald peacocks, each plaque joined by cabochon emerald links, French assay and hallmarks.......................**$1,495**

Bracelet, gold (14k multicolored), designed w/13 mottled "patchwork" plaques, each joined by small straight pins and highlighted w/two small sapphires and a diamond, hallmark for A.J. Hedges and Co., Victorian, ca. 1880s...........**$1,725**

Lapis lazuli and diamond bracelet, $2,300.

Bracelet, gold (14k yellow), flexible plaque design alternating round floret links w/concave barrel-shaped stations, ca. 1900...**$1,380**

Bracelet, gold (14k yellow), art nouveau-style, slide-type composed of 11 individual diamond-set female silhouettes...**$2,070**

Bracelet, gold (18k yellow), enamel and diamond, designed as a hinged flexible coiled snake, the body w/guilloché pink enamel and adorned w/six old mine-cut and rose-cut diamonds set in silver, enamel damaged, Victorian...**$4,750**

Bracelet, lapis lazuli and diamond, an open, flexible design w/six ornate sections, each centering a round cabochon-cut lapis lazuli capped w/a rose-cut diamond w/gold fleur-de-lis designs and rose-cut diamonds on each side, attached to round snake chain borders, mounted in 18k yellow gold, two diamond points missing, 7 1/4" l. (ILLUS. of part)..**$2,300**

Mourning bracelet, hair and enamel, a wide braided hair bracelet joined by a 14k yellow gold tongue-in-groove locket clasp highlighted w/jet black enamel w/yellow gold floral chased work decoration, hinged lid opens to view a painted miniature of a young girl within a landscape, scratch

Pearl, sapphire and diamond bracelet, $12,075.

from girl's hair down to her neck, ca. 1850, Victorian, 8 1/2"
l. **$460**

Bracelet, pearl, sapphire and diamond, flexible, strap type,
designed w/seven rows of natural seed pearls centering a
cushion-shaped, faceted sapphire, surrounded by a square
frame of 14 old mine- and old European-cut diamonds,
decorated w/three small rectangular-shaped plaques each
w/a centerline of square French-cut sapphires flanked by
two rows of small round diamonds, mounted in platinum
w/18k white gold catch, ca. 1900, approx. 6 1/2" l. (ILLUS.,
above)..**$12,075**

Bracelet, ruby, diamond and pearl, each section set w/
rubies in an "X" motif and centered by a row of old mine-cut
diamonds, enhanced by a border of old mine-cut diamonds
and pearls, one ruby missing, one section detached, lead
solder, silver mount. **$13,800**

Bracelet/brooch, gold, ruby and diamond, wide mesh
bracelet w/diamond accents w/detachable brooch of old
mine-cut diamonds and cushion-cut rubies, pinched collet
settings, ropetwist accents......................................**$5,750**

BROOCHES

Amethyst and diamond circle brooch, $1,645.

Brooch, aquamarine and diamond, centered by an emerald-cut aquamarine within an open wirework, millegrain and rose-cut diamond frame w/four green gold florets and collet-set aquamarine terminals, 14k yellow gold mount, Russian hallmarks, Edwardian, one diamond missing. **$2,990**

Brooch, amethyst and diamond, circle-form, designed w/ eight bezel-set round faceted amethysts spaced between 16 bead-set old European-cut diamonds, platinum-topped 14k yellow gold mount w/millegrain accents, partial number on back, Edwardian (ILLUS.). **$1,645**

Cameo brooch, carved shell, depicting the Three Muses, the center muse within a floral canopy, 14k yellow gold mount, Edwardian. **$460**

Cameo brooch, carved garnet, profile of a woman within a gold and silver mount, surrounded by 30 old mine-cut diamonds spaced by six pearls, French gold marks, removable back, signed at neck "LEBAS." **$7,475**

Brooch, cat's-eye chrysoberyl, memorial-type, bezel-set w/oval cabochon w/14k gold ropetwist frame, verso w/locket containing hair. **$382**

Cameo brooch, hardstone and gold, a tested 14k yellow gold oval frame composed of delicate chased C-scrolls enclosing a hardstone cameo carved in high-relief w/a profile bust of a classical woman, her hair dressed w/leaves and berries, a sleeping ram mounted on her shoulder, early 20th c., 1 3/4" x 2 1/4". **$1,725**

Cameo brooch, hardstone, oval, depicting a woman and cherub, surrounded by rose-cut diamonds within an ornate pierced 18k yellow gold mount, Victorian. **$2,645**

Cameo brooch, lava, the tested 10k yellow gold mount set w/a large pea green lava cameo carved in high-relief w/a profile cut of a classical woman, late 19th c., 1 1/2" x 1 3/4". **$748**

Brooch, reverse-painted crystal, round crystal reverse-painted w/a shore bird on grass on a mother-of-pearl background, within a diamond and millegrain 14k gold-

Reverse-painted crystal brooch, $2,585.

Diamond corsage brooch, $6,900.

topped platinum mount, Edwardian
(ILLUS. p. 71)..**$2,585**

Brooch, diamond, a floral and leaf design, decorated w/
old mine- and rose-cut diamonds, the five flowerheads en
tremblant, mounted in silver-topped 18k yellow gold, several
detachable sections, ca. 1830 (ILLUS. p. 71). **$6,900**

Brooch, diamond, garland-style decorated w/24 old mine-
cut diamonds and rose-cut diamonds, mounted in platinum,
ca. 1890, numbered w/French hallmarks and maker's mark
(ILLUS.)...**$2,990**

Diamond brooch, $2,990.

Art nouveau diamond brooch, $5,060.

Brooch, diamond, art nouveau-style, graceful openwork w/lozenge-shaped design centering a large old mine-cut diamond w/old mine- and rose-cut diamond accents, one small rose-cut diamond missing, mounted in platinum-topped 18k yellow gold (ILLUS.). **$5,060**

Brooch, diamond, bow design set w/173 rose-cut diamonds set in a platinum and 18k yellow gold mount, some diamonds missing to under-gallery, French hallmarks, No. 6113. .... **$6,900**

Brooch, diamond, bow and swag design set throughout w/bead and collet-set diamonds, platinum-topped 14k gold, Edwardian. **$4,255**

Brooch, diamond, flower design centered by a collet-set old European-cut diamond, surrounded by numerous collet and bead-set diamonds, platinum-topped 18k gold, signed "Marcus and Co.," Edwardian...............................**$19,550**

Brooch, diamond, pinwheel design set w/old European-cut diamonds, openwork 14k yellow gold mount..........**$2,990**

Brooch, diamond and emerald, modeled as a butterfly w/en tremblant wings set w/old mine and Swiss-cut diamonds and calibré-cut emeralds, the body also set w/emeralds and diamonds, ruby eyes and diamond-studded antennae, mounted in 18k yellow gold and platinum...............**$3,220**

Brooch, diamond and enamel, modeled as an eagle, the body designed w/pavé-set rose-cut diamonds, feathers and head decorated w/shaded guilloché enamel, talon suspending a pearl drop, silver-topped gold mount, French import mark..**$4,370**

Brooch, diamond and pearl, four-loop bow design set w/approximately 153 old mine-cut diamonds, suspending a natural pearl drop, diamond-set cap, silver-topped 18k yellow gold mount, European hallmarks..........................**$17,250**

Brooch, diamond, pearl and garnet, designed as a flowerhead, set w/a demantoid garnet surrounded by eight old European-cut diamonds, petals set w/diamonds, garnets and split pearls, 15k gold mount, Edwardian. **$3,335**

Brooch, diamond, pearl and platinum, flower basket design, openwork platinum grill surmounted by pearl and diamond flowers, set throughout w/41 round brilliant- and single-cut diamonds and 21 pearls in shades of pink, gray and cream, millegrain accents, minor gold solder, Edwardian. ...**$6,325**

Brooch, diamond and platinum, the circular openwork floral filigree design centering a round diamond, approx. .50 ct., additionally adorned w/204 round diamonds, total approx. 4.50 cts., signed "T.B. Starr," Edwardian, approx. 17.3 dwt. **$12,650**

Brooch, diamond, ruby, garnet, moonstone, gold and platinum, butterfly-shaped, the 14k yellow gold and platinum top openwork mount set w/two oval and one round cabochon moonstone weighing about nine carats surrounded by 42 old mine- and European-cut diamonds weighing about 1.15 carats, the eyes set w/two round faceted rubies weighing about .10 carats, the back of the head set w/one round faceted demantoid garnet weighing about .20 carats, early 20th c., 2" w. **$6,325**

Brooch, diamond, sapphire and 14k gold, gem-set model of insect, wings and body collet and bead-set w/29 rose, old mine- and old European-cut diamonds and 20 oval and

Emerald, gold and diamond brooch, $2,820.

circular-cut sapphires, ruby eye, rose gold legs and antennae, detachable silver-topped rose, gold mount. **$3,525**

Brooch, emerald and 18k yellow gold, a ribbon bow design set throughout w/square-cut emeralds, the gold frame enhanced w/floral engraving, ca. 1860. ....**$3,450**

Brooch, emerald, gold and diamond, concentric design of square- and emerald-cut emeralds set in crimped 18k gold bezels, further highlighted by rose-cut diamonds mounted in silver bezels (ILLUS.). **$2,820**

Art nouveau flower brooch, $2,350.

Brooch, enamel, art nouveau-style, designed as an orchid and decorated w/pale pink and yellow iridescent enamel, the stamen set w/two old European-cut diamonds and pearls, 14k gold mount, hallmark for Whiteside and Blank (ILLUS.). **$2,350**

Brooch, enamel, art nouveau-style, orchid design, purple, pink and green enamel petals accented w/an old mine-cut diamond, minor chip to enamel. **$1,610**

Brooch, enamel, 14k yellow gold, garnet, ruby and diamond, art nouveau-style dragonfly design w/green and white guilloché enamel wings edged w/seed pearls, demantoid

Art nouveau dragonfly brooch, $2,645.

garnet eyes, ruby and diamond accents, minor chips to enamel, hallmark for Riker Bros. (ILLUS.). **$2,645**

Brooch, enamel and diamond, model of butterfly, red, yellow, blue and black basse taille enamel wings and old mine-cut diamond body, ruby eyes, rose-cut diamond accents, silver-topped 14k gold mount, Austro-Hungarian hallmarks (ILLUS. p. 79)..**$6,463**

Brooch, enamel and diamond, young fair-haired woman depicted in three-quarter profile wearing a diadem w/star-set old mine-cut diamond against shades of lavender and

Enamel and diamond butterfly brooch, $6,463.

blue, framed by 28 old mine-cut diamonds, 18k gold mount, French guarantee stamp (ILLUS. p. 80)................ **$1,840**

Brooch, enamel and gold, Arts & Crafts-style, the freeform mount decorated w/polychrome enamel in green, lavender and gold in a flower and berry design, the reverse engraved "B.M.W.," designed by Louis Comfort Tiffany and signed by Tiffany and Co. (ILLUS. p. 81)..........................**$36,425**

Brooch, gold (14k) and diamond, stickpin-type bar w/ ribbon swags suspended by five antique and art nouveau full-cut diamond-set stickpin heads, diamond flowerhead

Enamel and diamond brooch,
$1,840.

surmount, stickpins w/hallmarks for "Carter, Howe and Co. and Dieges and Clust." **$646**

Brooch, gold (22k yellow), enamel and diamond, a floral engraved ribbon design w/blue enamel knot set w/old mine-cut diamonds, suspending a blue enamel locket, the scalloped edge accented w/gold and center-set w/diamonds set in a star shape, ca. 1860. ....**$4,025**

Brooch, gold (14k yellow) and gems, rectangular form set w/a clipped corner modified rectangular-cut tourmaline w/overall applied foliate and bead motifs, collet-set diamond and demantoid garnet accents, Edward Oakes, accompanied by copy of original drawing. **$7,015**

Arts & Crafts Tiffany enamel brooch, $36,425.

Brooch, gold and sterling silver, large curved cut-out blossom and leaf sprig design, England, Georgian era, late 18th-early 19th c. (ILLUS. p. 82). **$1,200**

Brooch, garnet and silver, silver circular-shape set w/nine garnets between enameled figures, ca. 1900 (ILLUS. p. 82). **$168**

Brooch, moonstone and enamel, art nouveau-style centered by an oval moonstone within a foliate blue green enamel and 18k yellow gold mount w/sapphire accents, signed "Tiffany and Co.," boxed. **$17,250**

Brooch, moonstone and sapphire, Arts & Crafts-style, four bezel-set moonstones joined by a foliate design of collet-set sapphires and seed pearls, 14k yellow gold, attributed to Edward Oakes (ILLUS. p. 84) **$2,645**

English Georgian silver and gold brooch, $1,200.

Victorian garnet brooch, $168.

Edwardian opal and diamond brooch, $1,293.

Brooch, opal and diamond, oval opal framed by seed pearls and old European-cut diamonds, 14k gold mount, Edwardian, hallmark for Krementz and Co., w/original Tiffany and Co. box (ILLUS.)..**$1,293**

Brooch, pearl, amethyst, aquamarine, ruby and gold, Arts & Crafts-style, wreath design centered by a prong-set oval amethyst cabochon surrounded by clusters of wire-set seed pearls and prong-set carved emerald leaves, faceted amethysts, lavender star rubies and aquamarines, silver mount wire gold bead accents, by Dorrie Nossiter, England (ILLUS. p. 85)..**$3,680**

Moonstone and sapphire brooch, $2,645.

Brooch, natural pearl and diamond, composed of three
rosettes, each centering a natural round pearl surrounded
by old mine-cut diamonds separated by diamond-set trefoil
designs, the center rosette suspending three large old mine-
cut diamonds in a free-hanging frame of small pearls and
diamonds w/a free-hanging old mine- and rose-cut diamond

Arts & Crafts jeweled brooch, $3,680.

accented bow design drop on either side, each terminating w/a pear-shaped pearl drop decorated at the top w/rose-cut diamonds, center portion detachable to be worn as a pendant, mounted in silver and silver-topped 18k yellow gold, three small rose-cut diamonds missing, ca. 1865..**$14,950**

Art nouveau fairy brooch, $2,016.

Brooch, pearl, diamond, 18k gold, plique-à-jour and enamel fairy-form, art nouveau-style, figure holds bouquet of enameled flowers w/center diamond, her body enameled, her wings of plique-à-jour set w/diamonds, a cultured pearl depends from the base of her dress, ca. 1900 (ILLUS.). **$2,016**

Brooch, pearl and diamond, Arts & Crafts-style, 14k white gold scrolled openwork rectangular mount w/diamond accents, set w/four freshwater petal-shaped pearls, two w/ lavender hue, radiating from a center pearl.................**$633**

Brooch, pearl and diamond, wing design center set w/a round old European-cut diamond surrounded by six seed pearls, the wings pavé-set w/split pearls, 14k yellow gold mount, ca. 1900, Victorian. **$1,093**

Brooch, pearl, emerald and ruby, designed as a coiled emerald and pearl-set serpent w/pearl in fangs, surmounting a starburst set w/rubies and pearls w/large center prong-set pearl, 18k yellow gold mount, English gold mark, solder to back, 19th c...**$1,725**

Brooch, platinum and diamond, bead and prong-set throughout w/76 rose, single, and full-cut diamonds, approx. total wt. 1.70 cts., French hallmark, Edwardian........$2,000

Brooch, platinum, diamond and onyx, stylized bow design w/a geometric onyx frame flanked by diamond-set terminals, set w/270 rose-cut diamonds, in a platinum-topped 18k yellow gold mount, French hallmark, Edwardian......**$6,325**

Brooch, plique-a-jour enamel, art nouveau-style, square openwork naturalistic design centered by three graduated fluted emerald beads within an 18k yellow gold green plique-a-jour frame w/diamond accents, probably originally a buckle, minor enamel loss, signed "Marcus and Co." (ILLUS. p. 88). **$18,400**

Brooch, plique-à-jour and green sapphire, circular form centering a bezel-set green sapphire within a green plique-a-jour lily pad design decorated w/wiretwist, 18k gold mount,

Plique-a-jour brooch, $18,400.

designed by Louis Comfort Tiffany, marked by Tiffany and Co., one bead detached, minor loss to plique, ca. 1910 (ILLUS. p. 89). **$4,113**

Brooch, ruby and diamond, art nouveau-style, an open frame w/a stylized wreath design centering a free-hanging oval faceted ruby flanked by two curved rows of old mine-cut diamonds topped w/an old mine-cut diamond, suspended from a pair of pearl-shaped faceted rubies and diamonds,

Plique-à-jour and sapphire brooch, $4,113.

the lower portion decorated w/six rectangular cushion-cut rubies slightly tapering in size, w/old mine- and rose-cut diamonds between the rubies and in the borders, mounted in platinum and 18k yellow gold, signed by Vever, Paris, ca. 1900. ....**$10,925**

Brooch, ruby, emerald, sapphire and silver, flower-form, the vermeil silver openwork mount set w/about 115 round faceted rubies weighing about 12 carats, the leafage set w/50 round, square and rectangular-cut emeralds weighing about 5 carats and six circular and cushion-cut blue sapphires weighing about .50 carats, second half 19th c., underside w/some solder repair, 3 3/4" l. **$1,725**

Brooch, sapphire and diamond, center prong-set cushion-shaped Kashmir sapphire surrounded by 10 prong-set old

Sapphire and diamond slide/brooch, $88,300.

mine-cut diamonds, platinum prongs w/18k yellow gold mount, brooch frame detaches to be worn as a slide, chip to girdle and surface scratches, Edwardian, accompanied by AGL Colored Stone Origin Report No. CS 32685, stating natural sapphire, Kashmir (ILLUS.)...................**$88,300**

Brooch, sapphire and diamond, double crescent design w/one crescent set w/10 cushion shape sapphires w/collet-set diamond accents, the other set w/17 old mine-cut diamonds, platinum mount, 14k white gold pin stem, signed "Yard" (ILLUS. p. 91)...**$4,715**

Double crescent brooch, $4,715.

Brooch, sapphire, diamond and 18k yellow gold, crescent-shaped design alternating round sapphires and diamonds, ca. 1900. ....**$2,070**

Brooch, sapphire, emerald, ruby and moonstone, Arts & Crafts-style wreath design w/prong-set faceted and cabochon sapphires, emeralds and moonstones and clusters of wire-set pearls, highlighted by a sapphire and ruby insect set in 14k yellow gold, gilded silver leaves and mount, by Dorrie Nossiter, England (ILLUS. p. 92).........................**$8,625**

Arts & Crafts jeweled wreath brooch, $8,625.

Sapphire and pearl brooch,
$1,410.

Brooch, sapphire and pearl, centered by an oval mixed-cut
  sapphire measuring approx. 14.20mm x 12.20 mm, framed
  by two rows of split pearls, 14k gold, closed back mounting,
  Edwardian, England, missing one pearl (ILLUS.). ... **$1,410**

Brooch, silver and malachite, Arts & Crafts-style, openwork
  design w/a bird highlighted by bezel-set round malachites, ca.
  1915-27, stamped 830 and signed "Georg Jensen, Denmark,
  No. 165." **$460**

Brooch, silver and enamel, Renaissance Revival-style, design
  of a nesting bird w/three chicks suspended from a garnet-
  set bar pin top, overall polychrome enamel decoration,
  Hungarian hallmarks, enamel loss, assayer's mark for 800
  silver. **$3,220**

Cameo brooch/pendant, citrine, diamond, pearl and
  enamel, Egyptian Revival-style w/center citrine cameo bust of

Egyptian Revival cameo brooch/pendant, $4,600.

woman w/Egyptian headdress, framed by rose-cut diamonds, pearls and orange, blue and white enamel, suspending five pearl and enamel drops, 18k yellow gold mount (ILLUS.). **$4,600**

Cameo brooch/pendant, carved shell, depicting "Three Graces" within narrow gold frame, Edwardian, 2 1/4" l. (ILLUS. p. 95)..**$325**

Brooch/pendant, diamond and pearl, ivy leaf design w/old mine- and rose-cut diamonds terminating in a baroque pearl, mounted in silver-topped 18k yellow gold, the end portions of the pendant are detachable to be worn as a

Edwardian cameo brooch/pendant, $325.

Diamond and pearl brooch/pendant, $5,750.

brooch, the original chain replaced w/14k white gold chain, one diamond missing (ILLUS.)............................. **$5,750**

Brooch/pendant, emerald, diamond and pearl, the garland-style decorated w/a laurel motif, centering a large emerald-cut Columbian emerald, framed by small old mine single-cut diamonds w/old mine single- and Swiss-cut diamonds in the floral and leaf designs, accented w/five natural pearls, diamond-set hinged pendant attachment at the top, removable brooch pin, mounted in silver-topped 18k yellow gold, ca. 1900, w/original fitted leather box. **$10,350**

Fine micromosaic brooch/pendant,
$1,064.

Brooch/pendant, micromosaic, an oval form w/a black
onyx ground inlaid w/the image of a walking peasant lady
in a red and white dress and shawl, in a 14k gold ropetwist
border mount, ca. 1850 (ILLUS.). **$1,064**

Brooch/pendant, pearl, enamel and gold,14k yellow
gold open-work form set w/14 seed pearls centered by an

Victorian flower brooch/pendant, $252.

*Diamond star brooch/
pendant, $2,530.*

enameled lavender pansy and green and leaf form centered
w/a seed pearl, ca. 1880 (ILLUS.)............................**$252**

Brooch/pendant, diamond, star form centered by old
mine-cut light yellow diamond, six old mine-cut diamonds
in buttercup settings between star points w/30 old mine-
cut diamonds set in star points, silver topped gold mount
(ILLUS.). **$2,530**

*Heart-shaped opal brooch/
pendant, $1,840.*

Brooch/pendant, opal and diamond, the prong-set
heart-shaped opal framed by a bead- and prong-set diamond
accented silver-topped 14k yellow gold pendant, detachable
pin back (ILLUS.)..**$1,840**

Brooch/pendant, diamond, pearl, garnet and sapphire,
set throughout w/multicolored natural pearls, fancy color
diamonds, pink stones, demantoid garnets and centering an
oval pink sapphire, platinum-topped 18k yellow gold, late
19th c., signed "Tiffany and Co." (ILLUS. p. 100)..**$63,000**

Tiffany jeweled brooch/pendant, $63,000.

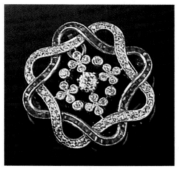

Ruby and diamond brooch/
pendant, $2,760.

Brooch/pendant, ruby and diamond, double knot design of bead-set diamonds and calibre-cut channel-set rubies centered by a prong-set old European-cut diamond, floret diamond accents, platinum-topped 14k yellow gold mount (ILLUS.). **$2,760**

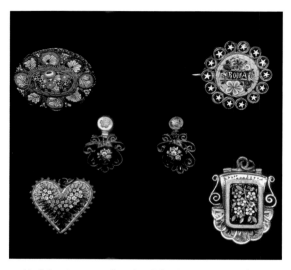

Top left: micromosaic brooch with floral design, c.1900, $125; top right: micromosaic brooch, c. 1880, $225; middle: gold-filled earrings with micromosaics, c. 1870, $195; bottom left: heart-shaped micromosaic pendant, c. 1880, $450; bottom right: gold-filled micromosaic watch fob, c. 1890, $395.

CHAINS

Platinum, pearl and sapphire bead chain, $3,525.

Chain, platinum, sapphire and pearl, bead chain designed w/10 sapphire beads flanked by freshwater pearls, joined by pierced navette-shaped links, Edwardian, England, 44" l. (ILLUS.). **$3,525**

CHATELAINES

Chatelaine, sterling silver, multi-hook design w/tiered filigree waist plaque incorporating cherubs w/a glass perfume bottle, pencil holder, needle case and egg-shaped thimble holder, English hallmarks, missing one appendage, ca. 1891. ....**$863**

COLLAR

Beadwork and silver collar, $3,565.

Collar, beadwork and silver, Arts & Crafts-style, composed of silver, gold, green and yellow beads designed as five square woven plaques w/floral design, each joined by six strands of beads, completed by a silver metal slide clasp, possibly Wiener Werkstatte, ca. 1908, 13" l., (ILLUS.). **$3,565**

CUFF LINKS

Cuff links, demantoid garnet and diamond, double-sided, each side w/a looped petal form centering a round faceted demantoid garnet w/small rose-cut diamonds set in the petals and borders, mounted in silver-topped 18k yellow gold, ca. 1895, pr. **$2,185**

Cuff links, gold (18k) and pearl, prong-set freshwater pearls connected by figure eight links, signed "Tiffany and Co.," ca. 1910..**$920**

EARRINGS

Earpendants, gold (14k) and turquoise cabochon, hemisphere and sphere design, bow and hanging tassel suspended, bezel and gypsy-set throughout w/turquoise cabochons, applied wirework accents, 10.5 dwt., Victorian (evidence of solder, small dents, missing elements).....**$104**

Earrings, chrysoberyl, golden yellow stones designed as flowerheads suspending similar drops, sterling silver mount, pr. **$2,530**

Earrings, coral, topaz, zircon, garnet and tourmaline, Arts & Crafts-style, designed as a cluster of prong-set faceted gemstones, including topaz, zircon, garnet and tourmaline, w/pearl and gold bead accents, surrounding a coral cabochon and suspending a carved coral pear-shape framing a gem-set drop, by Dorrie Nossiter, England, crack to one bottom stone, pr. (ILLUS. of one p. 107). **$2,070**

Earrings, diamond, gold and silver, 14k white gold and silver screw-back mount set w/two old mine-cut diamonds weighing about .20 carats suspending a yellow gold and silver top tassel set w/12 graduated old mine-cut diamonds weighing about .50 carats, last quarter 19th c., screw-back added later, pr...**$1,610**

Arts & Crafts jeweled earring, $2,070 for the pair.

Earrings, diamond, seed pearl, gold and platinum, a 14k yellow gold and platinum top mount w/an arched design and set w/11 rose-cut diamonds weighing about .15 carats and one seed pearl, suspending a basket of flowers tassel set w/four seed pearls and 25 rose-cut diamonds weighing about .30 carats, Edwardian, ca. 1910, 1" l., pr. **$2,300**

Earrings, emerald, diamond, pearl and gold, 18k yellow gold and silver top floral-design openwork mount set w/an oval faceted emerald weighing about .25 carats surrounded by 15 rose-cut diamonds suspending a bluish green cultured pearl tassel measuring 6.8 mm, tassel of later date, second half 19th c., 1 1/2" l., pr. **$316**

Earrings, enamel and gold, Persian design, gold ring hoop w/yellow metal bell-shaped drop w/three articulated tiers, enhanced by enamel and accented by white bead fringe, pr. **$1,150**

Earrings, gold (14k yellow), enamel and diamond, an old European-cut diamond set in the center of a round enamel gold-trimmed disk suspending an oval pendant enamel and gold foliate design, further suspending a small diamond-set drop, Victorian, pr. **$575**

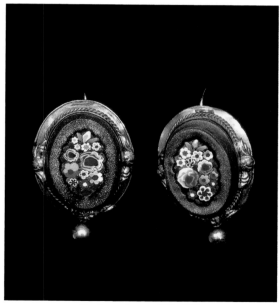

Mosaic earrings, c. 1880, $350.

Garnet earrings, c. 1900, $450.

HATPINS

Enamel violet hatpin, $518.

Hatpin, enamel, designed as a violet w/shaded pale pink enamel petals centered by a prong-set old mine-cut diamond, 18k yellow gold mount, gold-filled pin (ILLUS.). **$518**

LAVALIERES

Edwardian lavaliere, $1,265.

Lavaliere, diamond and platinum, a bow design surmounted by a foliate spray, suspending fringed flexible tails, set throughout w/round diamonds, platinum mount, minor gold solder to back, Edwardian (ILLUS.)...... **$1,265**

Lavaliere, morganite and diamond, rectangular morganite terminal, diamond-set bow motif shoulders, suspending a faceted pear-shaped morganite, collet-set diamond accents, completed by a fancy link platinum chain, Edwardian, 15 1/2" l. **$2,645**

LOCKETS

Locket, gold, an oval shape w/an applied design of gardening tools, a flower basket and a hat, engraved multicolor 18k gold, French hallmarks, in fitted box (ILLUS. p. 114)...... **$2,185**

Locket, gold and enamel, designed as a hand holding a movable fan, oval frame w/shell and foliate motifs centered by red stones and a pearl, verso w/glass compartment, Victorian. **$1,495**

Locket, pearl and ruby, a circular design w/h.p. signed portrait of a child on porcelain, surrounded by a row of cushion-shaped, faceted Burmese rubies, framed by a row of natural half pearls that taper in size, seed pearl and ruby accents, hair compartment on reverse, circular bail decorated w/six additional pearls, mounted in 14k yellow gold, ca. 1810, together w/original fitted leather box (ILLUS. p. 115)... **$2,415**

Locket pendant, gold (18k yellow), art nouveau-style, circular form depicting bust portrait of woman w/upswept hair and wearing a diamond melée choker, scrolled vine and floral border..**$1,380**

Locket and chain, gold (14k yellow), onyx, pearl and diamond, the barrel link chain set to the front w/six button-

Gold pendant locket, $2,185.

shaped natural pearls suspending a rose-cut diamond continuing to a rose-cut diamond bail, the oval locket set on the front and reverse w/oval black onyx tablets, the front w/a rose-cut diamond monogram and the reverse w/a Masonic emblem..**$977**

Pearl and ruby portrait locket, $2,415.

NECKLACES

Necklace, amethyst, Arts & Crafts-style, designed w/ graduating bezel-set oval amethysts and naturalistic links, completed by fancy links, attributed to Oakes, 16 1/2" l. **$3,680**

Necklace, amethyst, pearl and 14k gold, festoon-type, the pearl, amethyst, trace line and S-scroll chain suspending three pear-shaped amethysts hanging within pearl-set, shield-shaped drops, the center suspending a larger amethyst, Edwardian, 15 1/2" l...**$1,610**

Necklace, amethyst and pearl, choker-type, a 14k yellow gold single line necklace w/64 circular yellow gold links, each set w/a half seed pearl, the center w/five floral circular links, each set w/one half seed pearl surrounded by 12 smaller seed pearls suspending a removable 14k yellow gold floral pendant set w/a large oval faceted amethyst surrounded by 42 half seed pearls, joined by a 14k yellow gold rectangular box tongue-in-groove clasp set w/two half seed pearls, Europe, ca. 1900, 15 1/2" l. **$1,840**

Necklace, aquamarine, pearl and gold, Arts & Crafts-style, centering a large oval aquamarine framed by cabochon aquamarines and seed pearls, suspended from a fine triple curb link 14k gold chain highlighted by bezel-set rectangular-

Fine Arts & Crafts jeweled necklace, $5,875.

Exceptional diamond necklace, $36,800.

cut aquamarines, pearls and fancy links, 18" l. (ILLUS. of part p. 117).. **$5,875**

Necklace, diamond, art nouveau garland-style, set w/rose-cut and old mine-cut diamonds, intricately decorated w/laurel leaf and lotus flower motifs, suspending several drops, the largest terminating in a pear-shaped old mine-cut diamond, mounted in silver and platinum, Russia, w/original fitted wooden box, approximately 16" l. (ILLUS. p. 118).**$36,800**

Necklace, diamond, floral and ribbon design, decorated w/old mine- and rose-cut diamonds, w/navette-shaped links, open oval links and small lozenge-shaped, diamond-set links, the detachable pendant w/brooch conversion attachment, mounted in silver-topped 18k yellow gold, 17 1/2" l. **$3,680**

Necklace, diamond, graduating geometric scroll design links bead-set w/rose-cut diamonds, silver-topped 18k gold mount, 15 1/4" l. **$7,050**

Necklace, diamond and ruby, the central element designed w/graduating rose-cut floral pendants, some ornaments highlighted w/collet-set rubies, suspended by a ruby and fancy link chain, 10k gold mount, 14 1/2" l. **$4,025**

Necklace, enamel, art nouveau-style, lavender and green iridescent enamel flowers w/green, pink and white plique-a-jour enamel leaves, accented throughout w/rose-cut diamonds and pearls, 18k yellow gold mount w/later faux pearl chain. **$1,265**

Necklace, garnet, single strand gilt metal necklace w/34 graduated floral links, each set w/seven round faceted garnets, the center w/four floral and scrolling garland-work pendants and drops set w/round faceted garnets, Victorian, 16 1/2" l. **$1,093**

Necklace, garnet and diamond, openwork pendant set w/a demantoid garnet, further set throughout w/rose- and old mine-cut diamonds, suspending a pear-shaped rose-cut diamond drop, completed by fine platinum chains accented w/rose-cut diamond trefoils, Edwardian. **$6,038**

Necklace, gold (18k), diamond and enamel, art nouveau-style, delicate trace link chain w/figure of woman in blue enamel dress suspended, framed by curving branches w/pink and blue plique-a-jour enamel leaves, bezel-set w/seven old European-cut diamonds and bead-set w/rose-cut diamond highlights, freshwater pearl terminal, 18" l. **$4,935**

Necklace, gold (14k yellow), diamond and enamel, festoon design, the snake chain w/five gold beads suspending four snake chain loops alternating w/three navette-shaped pendants decorated w/ribbon design at top and mounted

Micromosaic necklace, $661.

Edwardian opal and diamond necklace, $3,760.

w/rose-cut diamonds within an enamel starburst, ca. 1860, Victorian. **$2,300**

Necklace, gold (14k), composed of oval wirework links w/floret and flattened bead accents, 18 1/4" l...............**$705**

Necklace, gold (14k yellow), Archaeological Revival-style, fringe design, trace link chain suspending graduated pendant drops, 15 1/2" l. **$1,610**

Necklace, gold (18k yellow), Victorian Etruscan Revival-style, barrel-shaped links suspending stylized ivy leaf drops threaded through a loop-in-loop chain, completed by a scarab clasp, 16" l. **$3,450**

Necklace, hardstone intaglio, Classical Revival-style, designed w/13 gem-set and hardstone oval intaglio seals depicting classical scenes and figures, suspended from a festooned 18k yellow gold chain, minor solder evident, ca. 1880....**$2,530**

Necklace, jade and enamel, Arts & Crafts-style, elliptical-shaped jade within conforming enamel scrolled links joined by trace link chains, similarly-set pendant suspending three jade drops, 18k gold, some enamel loss, signed "Tiffany and Co.," 18" l. **$31,050**

Necklace, jade and pearl, featuring five oval-shaped carved jadeite jade sections, bordered by a row of seed pearls and joined by a wire-wrapped bow-shaped link 14k yellow gold chain, 15" l. **$1,610**

Necklace, micromosaic and gold, depicting a dove on a branch w/pink and white flowers against a teal ground, within a 14k yellow gold frame w/wiretwist and beaded accents, later 14k box-link chain, damage to frame, 17" l. (ILLUS. p. 121)...**$661**

Necklace, opal and diamond, festoon-style, fancy platinum open and navette-shaped diamond links supporting a platinum-topped gold festoon drop set w/pear-shaped opals surrounded by old European-cut diamonds and a diamond bow swag design of later origin, mark of J. E. Caldwell and Co., Edwardian, 16 3/4" l. (ILLUS. p. 122). **$3,760**

Necklace, opal and 18k yellow gold, festoon-style, set w/four cabochon-cut opals in matrix w/bead and wiretwist decoration, suspending seed pearl tassels, completed by a trace link chain, 16" l. Edwardian..**$1,725**

Necklace, pearl, cultured, 101 white pearls graduated in size from 3.75-7.01 mm, completed by openwork 18k white gold barrel clasp w/diamond accents, Continental hallmark, 22" l. **$382**

Necklace, pearl, cultured, composed of 46 white pearls w/rose overtones measuring approx. 8.05-8.20 mm, completed

Pearl and diamond necklace, $9,775.

by 18k gold X-form clasp, signed "T and Co." for Tiffany and Co., w/original suede pouch, 16 1/4" l. **$2,233**

Necklace, pearl, latticework seed pearl design suspending a seed pearl fringe pendant w/onyx terminals and cap, further highlighted by collet-set circular- and rose-cut diamonds, completed by a pierced and millegrained platinum clasp accented w/rose-cut diamonds, Edwardian, needs restringing, missing some pearls, 32" l. **$2,875**

Necklace, pearl and diamond, alternating round and floret links centered by 19 pearls (probably natural) and set throughout w/rose- and old mine-cut diamonds, silver-topped 14k gold, converts into one 7" l. bracelet by detaching two elements, necklace 14 1/4" l. (ILLUS.). **$9,775**

Victorian gold and pearl necklace, $805.

Necklace, pearl and gold, pearl-set links w/a central fringe of floral motif drops, 14k yellow gold, later ropetwist chain, Victorian, 14 1/2" l. (ILLUS. of part). **$805**

Necklace, pearl and spinel, a strand of seed pearls suspending a fringe of mixed-cut oval red spinel drops surmounted by a prong-set pearl and further accented by three pearl drops, 18k yellow gold mount, 15" l. **$2,530**

Necklace, tourmaline, Arts & Crafts-style, the center oval plaque set w/graduated tourmalines surrounded by Montana sapphires and edged w/various color natural pearls, joined by a triple strand of 18k yellow gold chains, clasp signed "Tiffany and Co.," together w/extra links, in original Tiffany box. **$49,450**

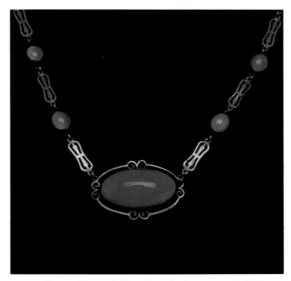

Sterling necklace with blue glass cabochons, c. 1910, $325.

Art deco necklace, sterling with enameling, c. 1920, $750.

PENDANTS

Cameo pendant, chalcedony, depicting the bust of a classical male within an oval blue and white enamel frame w/applied gold bead and wiretwist detail, 18k yellow gold mount, engraved "9th Decr. 1873" on reverse, minor chip to cameo, hallmark for Phillips Co. **$2,185**

Cross pendant, diamond, silver and gold, the ornate flattened cross in tested 14k yellow gold, the mount w/gold bead and rosette decoration and w/five relief silver floral designs each set w/a rose-cut diamond, suspended from a black silk ribbon, second half 19th c., 2" x 2 1/2". **$748**

Cross pendant, sapphires and 14k gold, gem-set cross w/circular-cut sapphires, cross suspended on gold chain w/ five square step-cut sapphires, bloomed gold mount, signed "Tiffany and Co.," 32" l. **$3,819**

Pendant necklace, diamond, art nouveau highly stylized butterfly-shaped outline w/delicate openwork, intricately set w/round- and rose-cut diamonds, one free-hanging in the center, mounted in platinum-topped 18k yellow gold w/double wire loops on the back w/white gold chain attached on each side, 17 1/2" h. (ILLUS. p. 130)..................**$4,830**

Art nouveau diamond pendant necklace, $4,830.

George IV pendant on chain, $532.

French diamond and opal pendant, $2,233.

*Etruscan Revival portrait
pendant, $1,725.*

Pendant and chain, diamond, five free-hanging pear-shaped loops graduated in size and set w/round diamonds, centering a free-hanging pear-shaped diamond suspended from a row of round diamonds, the outer loop terminating in diamond-set fringe which tapers in size, mounted in platinum, on a 14k white gold chain, ca. 1915.........**$9,200**

Pendant on chain, diamond, emerald, pearl and gold,14k gold, round w/leaf-shaped scrolling designs set w/10 rose-cut diamonds, three emeralds and a natural pearl, George IV, ca. 1820 (ILLUS. p. 131)............................**$532**

Pendant, black onyx and rose gold, mourning-type, inscribed "Charles Lord Southampton, obt 22 March 1797" and "George Lord Southampton, obt 24 June 1810," centering a glass compartment containing locks of hair, enameled crown design bail, early 19th c....................................**$259**

Pendant, diamond and opal, the peacock form centered by a circular-cut opal, set throughout w/seven old mine-cut and 60 rose-cut diamonds, platinum-topped 18k gold mount, French guarantee and import stamps (ILLUS. p. 131). **$2,233**

Pendant, enamel and gilt, portrait-type, miniature, Etruscan Revival-style, depicting two children in polychrome enamel, ropetwist, floral and beaded accents, locket back, gilt mount (ILLUS. p. 132)... **$1,725**

Pendant, enamel, pearl, diamond and 14k yellow gold, art nouveau-style, depicting a shaded anemone, highlighted by a bezel-set circular diamond and suspending a flexibly set baroque pearl, chips to enamel, hallmark. **$1,840**

Pendant, glass, art nouveau-style, triangular-form molded glass depicting lily flowers against an opaque background in golden colors, attached to a knotted silk cord, minor crack near loop hole, signed "Lalique". **$575**

Pendant, molded glass, diamond and pearl, art nouveau-style, a rectangular plaque of opalescent mold-blown glass w/a scene depicting a group of robed figures w/gold faces, within a frame of small rose-cut diamonds, the frame accented on each side w/a double rose-cut diamond, the diamond at the base suspending a natural pearl drop, mounted in silver-topped 18k yellow gold, signed by Lalique and w/French hallmark, w/original fitted box, ca. 1900. .... **$16,100**

Pendant, gold (18k yellow), art nouveau-style, circular form, one half w/relief-molded eagle depicted, detailed feathers and collet-set diamond highlights, openwork foliate design on other half, platinum-set rose-cut diamond and millegrain accents.. **$1,380**

Pendant, gold (14k), opal and enamel, art nouveau-style, oval opal framed by a pink guilloché enamel lotus design, two diamond accents, suspended by a 14k gold trace link chain, hallmark for Krementz and Co. (crack to opal)............**$705**

Pendant, opal and enamel, art nouveau-style, centered by an oval opal within an openwork foliate design in pink jubilee enamel, diamond and opal accents, signed "Mrs. Newman, Goldsmith and Court Jeweller, 10 Savile Row," some damage to opals, in fitted box. **$2,875**

Pendant, pate de verre, art nouveau-style, round medallion depicting a bouquet of hydrangea flowers, suspended by a sea green knotted silk cord, initialed "G. A-R." for Argy Rousseau ca. 1924. ....**$978**

Pendant, platinum, enamel and diamond, quatrefoil form, centering a disk of cobalt blue guilloché enamel surmounted by a diamond quatrefoil accent, within a rose- and full-cut diamond filigree mount, suspended from a fine trace link chain w/pearl accent, Edwardian. **$3,220**

Pendant, sapphire and diamond, snowflake design centered by a cushion-cut pink sapphire, surrounded by prong-set round pink sapphires and collet-set diamonds, rose-cut diamond accents, suspended from a pinch-set diamond bail, silver-topped 14k yellow gold. **$4,025**

Pendant, silver, ivory and coral, designed as cluster of silver leaves and scrolling tendrils w/two fluted ivory bellflowers

Imperial topaz and diamond pendant, $17,250.

suspended, accented by three coral beads, probably designed by Dagobert Peche, Wiener Werkstatte, Austria, early 20th c. **$3,525**

Pendant, topaz and diamond, bow form above oval mixed-cut Imperial topaz surrounded by old mine-cut diamonds, completed by a yellow diamond briolette, platinum-topped 14k yellow gold, minor abrasion, lead solder, one diamond missing, Edwardian (ILLUS. p. 136). **$17,250**

Pendant, turquoise, gold and diamond, the openwork cartouche outline and foliate motif frame set w/an oval Persian turquoise cabochon and two old mine- and round rose-cut diamonds, suspending a teardrop-shaped turquoise cabochon...**$1,265**

Cameo pendant/brooch, carnelian and tri-color 18k gold, a three-dimensional turbaned head accented by diamonds and framed by an arch w/columns, scroll and floral motifs, retractable bail, French hallmarks. **$1,955**

Cameo pendant/brooch, shell and garnet, 14k yellow gold lattice and beadwork decorated mount set w/a large oval cameo depicting a gladiator and a woman riding a horse-drawn chariot, cherub holding a cornucopia within a clouded field, the frame set w/seven oval buff top garnets, 3 1/2" x 4"..**$805**

Cameo pendant/brooch, shell and garnet, a carved shell cameo depicting a profile bust of a young classical woman and flowers, 14k yellow gold mount set w/33 round cabochon garnets, solder repair to clasp, Edwardian..**$1,093**

Pendant/brooch, bloodstone, rose-cut diamond, ruby and 18k gold, the oval bloodstone surmounted by a rose-cut diamond and cabochon ruby floral design within an 18k gold pierced, chased and engraved floral and foliate frame set w/rose-cut diamonds and rubies, French import stamp, Victorian. **$489**

Pendant/brooch, chalcedony intaglio, depicting Marcus Aurelius or Commodus flanked by a snake, goddess and Apollo, mounted in an 1850s 18k yellow gold enameled frame w/foliate bail, ruby accents, some enamel loss to bail, ca. 1820. ....**$2,415**

Pendant/brooch, chalcedony, ruby and enamel, oval chalcedony carved w/four intaglio classical figures within a Holbeinesque polychrome floral enamel frame set w/three circular cut rubies, 18k gold mount. **$1,840**

Pendant/brooch, diamond and 14k gold, starburst pendant/brooch set w/50 old mine-cut diamonds, 14k gold mount, hallmark for Krementz and Co., ca. 1900. ....**$2,990**

Tiffany starburst pendant/brooch, $7,168.

Pendant/brooch, diamond, bow design w/five loops, each set w/nine old mine-cut diamonds and centered by an old European-cut diamond, 18k gold mount, ca. 1895. .**$1,955**

Pendant/brooch, diamond and demantoid garnet, model of a leaf bead-set w/circular-cut demantoid garnets within a gold ring decorated w/nine bezel-set old mine-cut diamonds, platinum-topped 18k gold mount. **$3,055**

Pendant/brooch, diamond and 18k gold, starburst design, set w/55 old European-cut diamonds, 18k gold mount, signed "Tiffany and Co." (ILLUS.). **$7,168**

Pendant/brooch, diamond and gold, oval frame containing portraits of young girls painted front and back,

Diamond and sapphire pendant/brooch, $8,225.

silver-topped 18k gold mount designed as a bow set w/old mine-cut diamonds, Edwardian, England..................**$1,410**

Pendant/brooch, diamond, rectangular, centrally set w/three old European-cut diamonds and bordered by a filigree design pavé-set w/44 round, old European-cut diamonds, w/detachable diamond-set bail, mounted in platinum, ca. 1910. ....**$4,600**

Pendant/brooch, diamond and sapphire, centered by oval sapphire measuring approximately 10.10 x 7.85 x 5.05 mm,

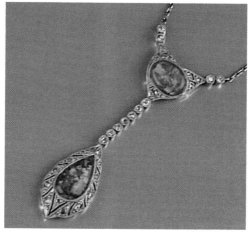

Black opal and diamond necklace, $3,525.

surrounded by 58 old mine, old European, and single-cut diamonds, approx. total wt. 5.56 cts., silver-topped 14k gold mount (ILLUS. p. 140)..**$8,225**

Pendant/compact, enamel and diamond, centered by a triangular neo-classical painted porcelain plaque depicting outdoor scene w/maidens, framed by single-cut diamonds, verso w/blue guilloché and white enamel decoration, opens to reveal two powder compartments, diamond-set bail, platinum-topped yellow gold, Edwardian. **$3,738**

Pendant/locket, gold (18k yellow), a shield-form pendant locket w/applied wiretwist detail and pearl accent, completed by a double oval link chain of reeded design w/14k rose gold six-pointed star decoration, the pendant and chain 18k yellow gold, some dents to back of locket, Victorian. **$1,725**

Pendant-necklace, black opal and diamond, delicate trace link chain suspending a pendant w/two bezel-set harlequin black opals and 31 bead and bezel-set single-cut diamonds, millegrain accents and pierced gallery, platinum-topped 18k gold mount, platinum chain, 16 1/2" l. (ILLUS. p. 141). **$3,525**

Pendant-necklace, gold (14k bi-color) and enamel, reeded trace link chain suspended by three foxtail tassel pendants and medallion w/enamel cherubs, all joined by swags, black tracery enamel accents, Victorian, 16 1/2" l. **$764**

Pendant-necklace, multi-stone and silver, Arts & Crafts-style, a carved rose quartz pendant capped w/bezel-set opals and faceted pink and lavender stones within a berry and leaf motif, suspended from a trace link chain, one opal chipped, 23 1/2" h. **$690**

Pendant-necklace, sterling silver and enamel, art nouveau-style, tripartite abstract-form pendant decorated en plein w/blue and green enamel, suspended from a baton-link chain, hallmarks for Chester, date letter for 1911, maker "C.H.," England. **$323**

Pendant-necklace, sterling silver and green agate, shaped pendant centered by an oval green agate, suspended from a silver paper clip chain, pendant stamped on reverse "TF (for Theodor Fahrner) - 935 -Déposé," 21" l....**$1,528**

PINS

Victorian gold bar pin, $1,035.

Bar pin, gold (15k yellow), navette-shaped, centered w/an octagonal-cut peridot, flanked on either side by foliate devices set w/half-pearls and two rubies, hallmarked "G," Victorian, w/fitted box (ILLUS.). **$1,035**

Bar pin, pearl, a row of natural pearls w/model of a bee at the center w/a natural pearl and faceted ruby body, ruby eyes and rose-cut diamond-set wings, the bee in silver-topped 18k yellow gold on an 18k yellow gold pin w/safety mechanism, ca. 1890. ....**$1,725**

Jabot pin, diamond and pearl, the top w/a natural pearl encircled w/rose-cut diamonds which extend and open up into a large circle of rose-cut diamonds (one old mine-cut), the base decorated w/a natural pearl and rose-cut diamonds, mounted in platinum, ca. 1908, numbered and signed "Cartier," Paris...**$2,990**

Rose-cut diamond serpent pin,
$1,058.

Pin, chalcedony (dyed), stylized lily designed w/ purplish gray chalcedony petals and green chalcedony leaves, rose-cut diamond stem, 14k white gold, Austro-Hungarian assay mark. **$1,265**

Pin, diamond and ruby, designed as coiled rose-cut diamond serpent w/ruby eyes, silver-topped, 14k gold mount, Austro-Hungarian hallmarks (ILLUS.). **$1,058**

Pin, diamond and seed pearl, designed as a diamond baton tied w/ribbon, bead-set w/59 old mine-cut diamonds, seed pearl and millegrain accents, silver-topped 18k gold mount, (ILLUS. p. 146). **$646**

Diamond and seed pearl pin, $646.

Pin, enamel and diamond, flying mallard w/basse taille enamel head, body and wings bead-set w/old mine, rose and single-cut diamonds, silver-topped 18k gold mount, w/fitted Asprey box. **$1,880**

Pin, garnet and diamond, a collet-set demantoid garnet w/diamond and pearl accents, further rose-cut diamond and platinum decoration, 14k yellow gold mount, Edwardian (ILLUS. p. 147). **$1,840**

Pin, gold (14k), art nouveau design depicting a profile of a woman within a naturalistic motif, diamond and ruby accents.................................... **$2,990**

Pin, gold (18k) and diamond, art nouveau-style, designed as griffin clutching an old European-cut diamond, rose-cut diamond accents, marker's mark "GC" **$2,350**

Pin, gold, enamel and diamond, modeled as a butterfly w/body and wings set w/old European-cut

diamonds, wings decorated in shaded orange guilloché enamel, black and white enamel accents..............................**$1,265**

Pin, pearl and diamond, crown design, the points set w/two old European-cut diamonds and three white and gray pearls, the gallery in an alternating pattern of four old European-cut diamonds and three purple, rose and golden-pink pearls, edged by collet-set old mine- and rose-cut diamonds, 18k gold mount. **$4,025**

Edwardian demantoid garnet pin, $1,840.

RINGS

Arts & Crafts garnet and pearl ring, $3,290.

Diamond ring, $764.

Ring, cat's eye, gentleman's, centered by a round double-sided cabochon chrysoberyl, 14k yellow gold dragon motif mount, ca. 1910. ....**$9,200**

Ring, demantoid garnet and pearl, Arts & Crafts-style, centering a circular-cut bezel-set green demantoid garnet flanked by seed pearls, the shoulders accented by gold and foliate designs, 14k gold mount, hallmark "MR" for Margaret Rogers, size 6 3/4 (ILLUS.).....................................**$3,290**

Ring, diamond, floret composed of nine old mine-cut diamonds weighing approx. 0.89 cts., scrolling openwork white metal and 18k yellow gold mount, English karat stamp, size 2, shank indistinctly inscribed (ILLUS. p. 148)......**$764**

Ring, diamond solitaire, an old mine-cut diamond weighing approx. 6 cts., mounted in platinum.....................**$16,675**

Ring, diamond, set w/two old European-cut diamonds, diamond-set platinum mount.............................**$20,700**

Ring, diamond, three stone navette shape, centered by a cinnamon color circular-cut diamond, further enhanced w/similarly cut yellow and colorless diamonds, flanked by diamond trefoils and swags, platinum-topped 18k gold, obliterated hallmark, possibly for Tiffany and Co., Edwardian...**$14,950**

Ring, diamond, silver and gold, dinner-type, the tested 14k yellow gold and silver top floral openwork mount set w/one old mine-cut diamond weighing about .50 carats surrounded by 48 smaller old mine-cut diamonds weighing about 2.25 carats, last quarter 19th c., size 7 1/2.....................**$1,150**

Ring, gold (14k bicolor), crystal, diamond and sapphire, the rose and yellow gold mount w/a carved frosted crystal depicting a young child's face wearing a bonnet set w/six old mine-cut and one round brilliant-cut diamond, ribbon below the child's chin set w/11 rose-cut diamonds, shank portion of ring is of a later date, ca. 1900................................**$1,265**

Fine antique emerald and diamond ring, $8,225.

Ruby and diamond ring, $5,750.

Ring, gold (14k yellow), platinum and diamond, filigree platinum reticulated mount set w/41 old mine- and old European-cut diamonds, ca. 1910, Edwardian. **$1,265**

Ring, emerald and diamond, centering an emerald-cut emerald measuring approx. 9.36mm x 8.14mm x 5.13 mm and weighing approx. 2.87 cts., flanked by old mine-cut diamonds, approx. total weight .92 cts., 18k yellow gold mount, England, size 5 (ILLUS.). **$8,225**

Ring, pearl and diamond, the center vertically set w/three pearls further set w/four collet-set diamonds and old European-cut diamond trefoils, platinum-topped 14k gold mount, Edwardian, w/finger guard...........................**$2,645**

*Sapphire and diamond
ring, $11,500.*

Ring, ruby and diamond, art nouveau-style, bezel-set w/
faceted cushion-shaped ruby measuring approx. 6.05 x 5.55
x 4.06 mm, flanked by old European-cut diamonds, approx.
total wt. 1 ct., scrolling foliate 18k gold mount, size
7 1/4...**$4,406**

Ring, ruby and diamond, art nouveau-style floral design
w/center-set ruby and three old mine-cut diamonds mounted
in silver and 14k pink and green gold, Russian hallmark, ca.
1900. ....**$1,265**

Ring, ruby and diamond, centered by a collet-set oval
ruby framed by crimped collet-set old mine-cut diamonds,
mounted in silver, surface scratches to ruby, later 14k white
gold shank (ILLUS. p. 150). **$5,750**

Ring, sapphire and diamond, a prong-set modified pear-
shaped sapphire within a heart-shaped frame set w/old mine-
cut diamonds in platinum, diamond-set shoulders, 18k yellow
gold shank, European hallmarks (ILLUS.). **$11,500**

Arts & Crafts jeweled cluster rings, $978 and $2,415.

Ring, peridot, citrine and aquamarine, Arts & Crafts-style, the bombé design featuring a prong-set round peridot surrounded by seven prong-set citrines and seven smaller aquamarines, gold bead accents, silver gilt mount, by Dorrie Nossiter, England (ILLUS. right) **$978**

Ring, sapphire, pearl and aquamarine, Arts & Crafts-style bombé design featuring a prong-set oval sapphire surrounded by eight prong-set round aquamarines and eight square-cut sapphires, seed pearl and gold bead accents, silver gilt mount, by Dorrie Nossiter, England (ILLUS. left) **$2,415**

Ring, silver and yellow gold, cat's eye and diamond, slave's ring set w/an oval cabochon cat's eye framed by 10 rose-cut diamonds and flanked on shoulder by relief-molded Turkish slave wearing a belt set w/a rose-cut garnet, one garnet missing, ca. 1840 ....**$575**

SETS

Bar pin and earrings, malachite and 18k gold, the three-dimensional pin enhanced w/wire twist and bead terminals suspending a cube-shaped drop, together w/ matching pair of earrings, Victorian, the set. **$546**

Brooch and earrings, gold (18k), the shield-shaped brooch designed w/overlapping gold sections accented w/seed pearls and amphora-shaped drops, matching earrings, Swedish import assay marks, Victorian, the set. **$1,265**

Brooch and earrings, gold (18k yellow) and mosaic, the brooch a rectangular form w/scroll and leaf design suspending a circular micromosaic plaque w/scarab design, together w/pair of matching earrings, ca. 1860, the set. **$1,955**

Brooch and earpendants, enamel, diamond, gem-set demi-parure, brooch w/flexible plaques decorated w/golden basse taille enamel and bezel-set w/five circular-cut citrines and 10 old European-cut diamonds, pear-shape faceted citrine terminal, 18k gold mount, signed "Marcus and Co.," the set. **$9,400**

Brooch/pendant and earrings, gold and turquoise, the brooch pendant an engraved scroll form surmounted

Sapphire and diamond brooch and earring, $7,763.

by pavé-set turquoise and seed pearl decoration, fine link chain suspending scrolled gold drop w/two further cone-shaped drops, together w/pair of earrings of similar design, Victorian, the set. **$920**

Brooch/pendant and earrings, sapphire and diamond, the brooch centered by a prong-set pear-shaped mixed-cut sapphire within a diamond-set scroll design surmounted by a pearl, suspending a prong-set pear-shaped sapphire drop, retractable bail and detachable frame for brooch clasp, platinum-topped 14k yellow gold mount, together w/a matching pair of earrings, dated 1903, Edwardian, the set (ILLUS. of part). **$7,763**

Earrings and pendant, diamond, the earrings each centrally set w/an old mine-cut diamond surrounded by 10 smaller old mine-cut diamonds, the pendant-drop set w/an old mine-cut diamond solitaire attached to a fine curb link 16" l. chain, mounted in 18k and 14k white gold, the set...**$5,405**

Necklace, bracelet and earrings, enamel, pearl and gold, consisting of French hallmarked 18k yellow gold serpent and leaf necklace, the leaves highlighted w/green enamel, alternating w/openwork serpent links suspending a removable serpent and leaf pendant-brooch w/four leaves highlighted w/green guilloché enamel centering a floral-designed set w/five baroque and one simulated pearl (one pearl missing), w/a matching bangle bracelet and earrings, last quarter 19th c., necklace 15" l., set of 4. ....**$1,840**

Necklace and earrings, citrine and pearl, festoon design set w/four pear-shaped buff-top citrines w/seed pearl and circular link chains, small diamond accents, 15" l., together w/matching earrings, platinum mounting, Edwardian...**$1,380**

Necklace, earrings and belt buckle/brooch, gold (18k bicolor) and enamel, parure comprising a necklace w/detachable pendant, day/night earpendants and belt buckle/ brooch, all matching pieces w/fruit and floral motif basse taille

18k gold "Placque de Cou," $49,938.

enameling w/acorn gold highlights, 18k yellow gold w/18k green gold inlay, French hallmarks, in original fitted leather box, the set. **$8,625**

Necklace and locket/brooch, garnet, the necklace a single strand base metal design w/32 floral links set w/rose-cut garnets suspending a base metal pear-shaped locket set w/round and pear-shaped rose-cut garnets, verso an open-hinged compartment, together w/a base metal floral locket/brooch set w/round and pear-shaped rose-cut garnets, verso an open compartment, Victorian, necklace 18" l., the set. **$1,380**

Necklace plaques, gold (18k), diamond and turquoise "Placque de Cou," art nouveau design, largest 2" x 7" rectangular curved openwork plaque centered w/carved turquoise woman's head w/chased flowing gold hair highlighted by old European-cut diamond blossoms, signed "Lalique," similar 2" square plaque also w/carved turquoise head and signed "Lalique," also a pair of smaller openwork plaques set w/diamond blossoms, accompanied by 18k gold flattened baton link chain, 20 1/2" l., two gold satin ribbons, one gold satin cord, and two screwdrivers, may be worn as chokers or necklaces, one plaque w/brooch fitting, the set (ILLUS. of largest plaque p. 156). **$49,938**

MISCELLANEOUS

Tiara, diamond, Belle Epoque-style, laurel leaf and ribbon garland design w/a large diamond free-hanging near the top and further decorated w/329 old mine- and rose-cut diamonds, mounted in silver-topped 18k yellow gold, gold-plated silver hair band, central portion is detachable, as well as the diamond drop, and can be worn as a ribbon and wreath designed brooch, ca. 1890, w/leather box. **$23,000**

Collecting Costume Jewelry

By Leigh Leshner

The first rule of collecting is to collect what you like! Don't worry about trends or what's the hot new collectible. Focus on amassing a collection that makes you smile, intrigues you, and inspires you. Let your imagination run wild. The possibilities are endless. A collection can consist of bird pins, bracelets, or jewelry made by a particular designer or design style. After that, focus on condition and quality. Is the piece well made? Is it missing any stones or pieces? Can the piece be repaired, and how much will the repair cost? These are all questions that you need to ask yourself when you are purchasing a piece of jewelry. But remember to enjoy yourself. Part of the fun is the thrill of the hunt, and finding that one piece that makes your heart stop!

Helpful Hints

• Be conscious of the piece's condition because it will affect its value. If the stones are yellowed, dark, or missing, the value and the price should not be comparable to pieces that are in excellent to mint condition.

• Unless a piece is rare or is one that you truly desire, think twice before purchasing an item that is not in good condition. However, if you are able to repair the piece yourself or through a jeweler, and the price is reflective of the condition, then it might be worthwhile to purchase.

• To be considered in excellent condition, the piece should have all of the stones and component parts, e.g., no missing or broken clasps, settings, or findings.

• Often, there is leeway in terms of condition when it comes to enameling. Over the years, enameling will become a bit worn. This means slight age wear, not chips and severe wear.

• Don't be talked into buying a piece of jewelry simply because it is signed. Just because a piece of jewelry is signed does not mean that it is more valuable. This is a myth that seems to be continually perpetuated. There are many pieces in the market that are unsigned and just as valuable as signed pieces. At the same time, there are signed pieces that have little value at all. So do not base your purchase merely on the fact that it is signed.

• Do not accept excuses for low-quality jewelry. I have often heard dealers tell customers that missing stones, yellowed stones, and broken pieces are acceptable because that is a sign of age. This is a sign of damage, and you should not be talked into accepting damaged goods based upon this excuse.

• Be aware that when a piece of jewelry is a popular item, the price may be artificially high and have no bearing on the intrinsic value.

• Take your time to examine the piece. Use a loupe to look for signatures and other marks as well as damage.

Costume Jewelry
BRACELETS

Bracelet, antique gold-plated links, four large ornate links set w/large faux gemstones and trimmed w/multicolor rhinestones, signed "Marino," 2 3/8" w. ....**$80-$100**

Bracelet, bangle-type, gold plate, hinged, top set w/clear rhinestones, 1" w. .... **$50-$70**

Bracelet, bangle-type, gold plate, ribbed design, signed "Ciner," 3/4" w. .... **$50-$75**

Bracelet, bangle-type, hinged, gold-plated, matte finish, squared top, purple marquise rhinestone designs, signed "Monet," 1 1/2" w. (ILLUS. p. 163). .... **$150-$175**

Bracelet, bangle-type, sterling, hinged w/safety chain, no decoration, Mexico, 1" w. .... **$65-$80**

Bracelet, bangle/watch, hinged, textured gold-plated finish, large faux emerald center w/marquise cabochon faux gemstones, opens to reveal watch under emerald center (ILLUS. p. 164)... **$185-$220**

Bracelet, brass, link-type, w/six large figural brass rose charms, ca. 1900... **$45-$65**

Monet bangle bracelet, $150-$175.

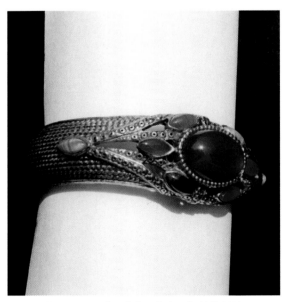

Faux gemstone bangle bracelet/watch, $185-$220.

Vendome charm bracelet, $65-$90.

Pot metal bangles, left to right: with blue rhinestones,
$66; hinged with blue and clear rhinestones, $68;
and hinged with clear and blue rhinestones, $115.

*Filigree bangles, from left: with amethyst rhinestones, $145;
with blue rhinestone, $110; with green and clear rhinestones,
$165; and with clear and blue rhinestones, $115.*

*Rhodium hinged bangle with clear rhinestones, pink, blue,
and green faceted glass, as well as red cabochons, $595.*

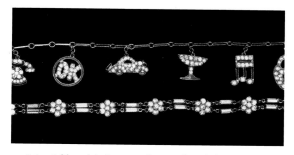

Pot metal bracelets, from top: charm style with clear rhinestones and enameling, $145, and with clear rhinestones, $98.

Pot metal hinged bangles, from left: with clear and blue rhinestones, $185; flower design with clear rhinestones, $225; and with clear and green rhinestones, $165.

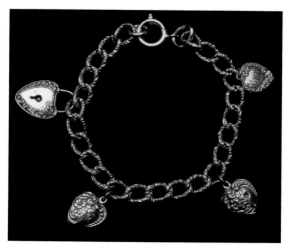

*Bracelet with heart charms and green
rhinestones and blue cabochons, $295.*

Gold-filled hinged bangles, from top: with open-back purple rhinestones, $245, and art nouveau with blue rhinestone, $165.

Expandable gold-filled bracelets, from top: one with clear rhinestones and blue faceted glass, $245, and the other with clear rhinestones and red open-back rhinestone, $355.

Bangles, from top: celluloid with clear rhinestones, $225;
celluloid with blue rhinestones, $185; celluloid with blue and
clear rhinestones, $165; Bakelite with red rhinestones, $185;
and Applejuice Bakelite with topaz rhinestones, $110.

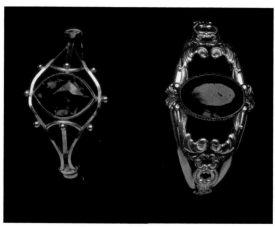

*Left: gold-filled hinged bangle with amethyst glass,
c. 1910, $165; right: gold-filled hinged bangle with
amethyst glass, marked FM Co., c. 1910, $155.*

*Yellow-metal hinged bangle with faceted glass, applied
flowers, and leaves, c. 1910, $275.*

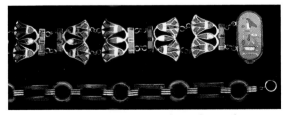

*Top: Egyptian revival bracelet, sterling with enameling,
c. 1925, $425; bottom: art deco slave bracelet, sterling,
green glass, and enameling, c. 1925, $225.*

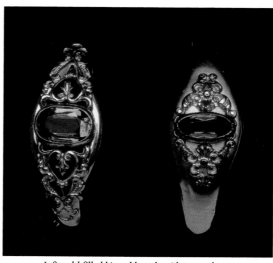

Left: gold-filled hinged bangle with topaz glass, c. 1910, $155; right: gold-filled hinged bangle with blue glass, marked FM Co., c.1910, $155.

Bracelet, charm, gold-plated multichain, filigree enclosed red beads, green "jade style" beads, basket style charm of green "jade" beads, red rhinestone trim, signed "Vendome" (ILLUS. p. 165)... **$65-$90**

Bracelet, charm, brass, chain w/six rose charms (ILLUS. p. 179)... **$55-$75**

Bracelet, gold-filled, large citrine color emerald cut glass stone in center, w/red baguettes rhinestones and clear round rhinestones on the sides, pink gold Retro design on the sides w/double snake chains, 1" w. in center. (ILLUS. p. 180)... **$325-$350**

Bracelet, gold-filled, link-type, hinged, five links w/oval shell cameos on scalloped center pieces, each link w/borders of cylinders and twisted metal, signed "Sammarti no Bros. Providence," ca. 1910, 1" w. .... **$375-$400**

Bracelet, gold plate, link-type, set w/individual multicolored carved glass scarabs, 1/2" w............................ **$55-$70**

Bracelet, gold plate, linked chain w/10 varied charms decorated w/blue, green and turquoise enamel...... **$40-$60**

Bracelet, gold-plated hinged links, large oval and octagonal purple art glass stones set on filigree and plain links, 1 1/8" w. (ILLUS. p. 180)... **$175-$200**

Bracelet with rose charms, $55-$75.

Gold-filled citrine colored emerald bracelet, $325-$350.

Gold-plated and art glass bracelet, $175-$200.

Art deco rhinestone bracelet, $175-$200.

*Goldtone bracelets, from top: with green and topaz
rhinestones, $90; with topaz and citrine rhinestones,
$95; and with topaz and citrine rhinestones, $88.*

From left: pot metal bracelet with green, blue, and aurora borealis rhinestones, $98, and open-back blue rhinestone bracelet, $265.

Bracelet, rhinestone, art deco-style, triple row open back set w/individual blue oval crystal stones, clear round, baguette rhinestone clasp, signed "Czechoslovakia," 5/8" w. (ILLUS. p. 181)... **$175-$200**

Bracelet, rhinestone and metal, expansion-style, white metal bracelet completely covered w/large emerald-cut clear rhinestones, 1/2" w. .... **$85-$100**

Bracelet, rhinestone and white metal, link-type, decorated w/clear stones and large marquise-shaped center stones, 5/8" w.. **$50-$70**

Bracelet, sterling silver, links of flower and leaves motif, signed "G. Cini," 1" w. (ILLUS. p. 184). .... **$250-$275**

Bracelet, sterling silver, link-type, w/connected curved ribbed leaves, signed "Jewelart," 1/2" w. .... **$55-$75**

Bracelet, sterling silver, link-type, w/enamel on sterling Pekinese dog charm, 1930s. .... **$55-$75**

Bracelet, sterling silver, link-type, w/matching sterling cat charm, 1950s, 1/4" w. .... **$45-$65**

Bracelet, sterling silver and rhinestone, late Retro-style, openwork design of ribbons/scrolls in rectangular panels linked together, entirely set w/clear rhinestones, signed "Unicraft Sterling," 1 3/8" w. (ILLUS. p. 185).... **$175-$195**

Cini floral bracelet, $250-$275.

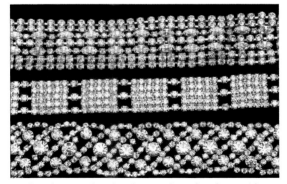

Clear rhinestone bracelets, from top down: $90, $88, and $95.

Sterling bracelet with rhinestones, $175-$195

Sterling silver snake upper-arm bracelet with clear and green rhinestones, $185.

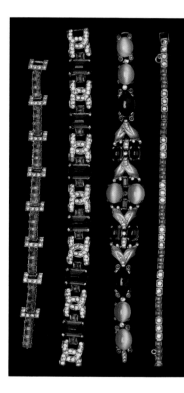

Assorted bracelets, from left: pot metal buckle with clear and red rhinestones, $185; sterling with blue, clear, and red rhinestones, $185; Trifari with red and clear rhinestones along with red and blue cabochons, $245; and sterling with red and clear rhinestones, $168.

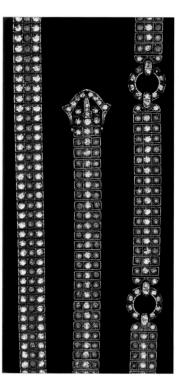

Three sterling Diamond Bar bracelets, all with clear and blue rhinestones, priced left to right: $295, $285 (also has buckle), and $245.

Bracelets, all with clear and green rhinestones, left to right: rhodium, $245; pot metal, $265; and ALL Co., $295.

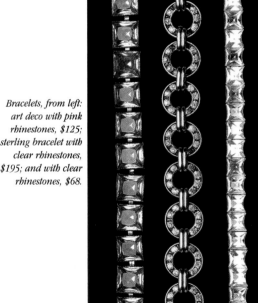

*Bracelets, from left:
art deco with pink
rhinestones, $125;
sterling bracelet with
clear rhinestones,
$195; and with clear
rhinestones, $68.*

Bracelets, from left: with red rhinestones, $145, and sterling vermeil with red cabochons and clear rhinestones, $195.

From top: bracelet with pink rhinestones and faux pearls, $85, and goldtone bracelet with faux pearls and citrine rhinestones, $145.

Bracelet, turquoise and metal, assorted real turquoise nuggets strung on elastic w/white metal textured spacer beads, 1/2" w.. **$70-$90**

Bracelet with clear rhinestones and blue, yellow, red, and green glass balls, $185.

Gold-filled hinged bangle with rhinestones, c. 1900, $195.

Art deco bracelet, Germany, sterling with enameling and molded glass, c. 1920, $650.

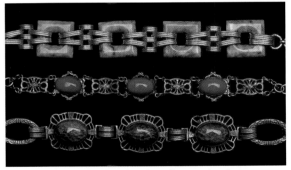

Top: Czechoslovakian bracelet, yellow metal and green glass, c. 1925, $225; middle: Czechoslovakian bracelet, brass, enameling, and red glass, c. 1925, $125; bottom: Czechoslovakian bracelet, brass and green glass, c. 1925, $150.

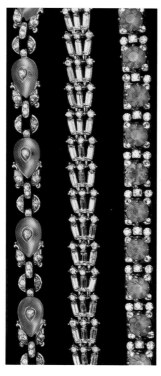

Bracelets, from left: Trifari with clear rhinestones and pink cabochons, $155; Trifari with clear rhinestones, $145; and sterling with clear rhinestones and blue faceted glass, $325.

BROOCHES

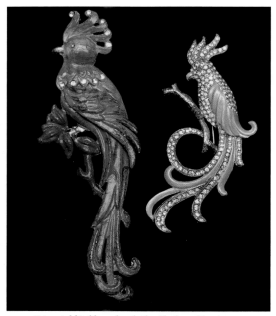

*Pot metal bird brooches, both with clear rhinestones
and enameling, priced from left: $98 and $125.*

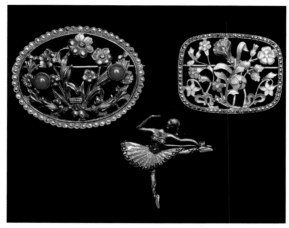

Marcasite brooches, clockwise from top left: pot metal with green cabochons, $95; sterling with enameling, $125; and sterling ballerina with enameling, $90

CHATELAINES

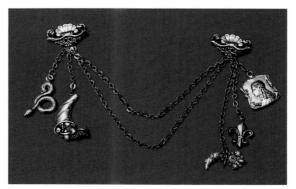

Chatelaine with Victorian-style charms, $100-$125.

Chatelaine, silver plate, Victorian motif charms suspended
   from two shell motif pins connected w/chains, ca. 1940s
   (ILLUS.).. **$100-$125**

CLIPS

Clip, dress-type, 935 grade sterling and rhinestone, large clear baguettes and marquise stones in center, openwork sides set w/small clear rhinestones, 1 3/4" h. ....**$90-$120**

Clip, dress-type, antiqued gold plate, leaf shape w/openwork flowers in center, each flower set w/blue, white or turquoise center, signed "NE," 1 7/8" x 2 1/2". ....**$40-$50**

Clip, dress-type, antiqued gold plate and rhinestone, curved ribbon shape, open work metal decorated w/four center handset large oval red rhinestones in graduated sizes, from large on top to small on bottom, each surrounded by clear rhinestone trim, 1 1/4" x 3 1/4". ....**$ 85-$110**

Clip, dress-type, copper-finish metal and glass, ornate filigree and etched design decorated w/large pink art glass oval stone on top, 2" x 2 1/2". ....**$50-$75**

Clip, dress-type, gold plate, glass and rhinestone, large spray of three gold bell-shaped flowers w/large center amber crystal centers and pavé clear rhinestone petals and stem, 2" x 3 1/2" (ILLUS. p. 200). ....**$75-$100**

Clip, dress-type, goldtone metal, openwork kite-shaped design studded w/large purple, pink, aqua, yellow, green and clear rhinestones, 1 3/4" x 2 1/4" (ILLUS. p. 201). ....**$55-$75**

Amber flower dress clip, $75-$100.

Dress clip of multicolored rhinestones, $55-$75.

Multicolored cabochon dress clip, $70-$90.

Clip, dress-type, goldtone metal, oval openwork design w/large oval red cabochon stone in center surrounded by panel w/leaf decoration and four smaller round multicolored cabochon stones in rope-twist border, an outer panel decorated w/fleur-de-lis and 12 oval multicolored cabochon stones, 2 1/4" x 2 1/2" (ILLUS. p. 202)....................................**$70-$90**

Clip, dress-type, rhinestone, floral motif set w/large blue, red, green and yellow marquise stones around green domed center, 1 3/4" d. ....**$35-$50**

Clip, dress-type, rhinestone, green crackle glass center stone inside frame of pink cabochons, upper bottom rows of pink, green, yellow and blue rhinestones, lower bottom row of five ribbon-style designs set w/tiny blue, red and purple cabochons, three hanging blue glass cone shapes, 2 1/2" x 2 3/4"...**$65-$85**

Clip, dress-type, rhinestone, inverted triangle shape, large pink oval rhinestones in openwork design w/matching channel-set square rhinestone borders and accents, 1 5/8" x 2 3/4"..**$65-$85**

Clip, dress-type, rhinestone, openwork metal completely set w/ clear rhinestones in art deco design, center large clear marquise stone w/red, emerald green and blue etched glass leaves above and below, small black enamel accents, 1 1/2" x 2"...**$70-$95**

Black and clear rhinestone dress clip, $75-$100.

Unusual art deco clip, $35-$50.

Clip, dress-type, rhinestone, three vertically stacked large round black stones framed by slightly smaller clear oval and marquise rhinestones, signed "Doctor Dress," 2" x 2 1/2" (ILLUS. p. 204). ....**$75-$100**

Clip, dress-type, white metal and glass, open work design completely set w/pale blue faux moonstones, clear rhinestone trim between stones, 1 3/4" x 2 1/4". .... **$70-$90**

Clip, dress-type, white metal and rhinestone, ornate openwork rococo design w/double swag chains and large oval clear and pink rhinestones in center, signed "Doctor Dress," 2 1/4" x 3". ....**$75-$100**

Clip, enamel, gold-plated art deco-style pen point, 2" (ILLUS. p. 205). .... **$35-$50**

Clip, fur-type, gold plate, glass, enamel and pearl, floral spray design w/pink, green, blue and purple glass squares forming flowers, a single side spray of graduated pearls, a light pink enameled bow at bottom, 2 1/4" x 3 3/4". .... **$100-$120**

Clip, fur-type, gold plate, glass and enamel, spray design of three flowers w/large amber rhinestone centers, small clear rhinestone trim, navy blue enamel ribbon at top, signed "Trifari," 2 5/8" h. ....**$125-$150**

Clip, fur-type, gold plate, sword design w/filigreed hilt set w/large red cabochon on top, smaller red, green and blue

*Flower fur clip, enameling with clear rhinestones
and pink cabochons, c. 1935, $145.*

Gold plate and glass art deco clips, $135-$160.

cabochons on border and at center, signed "Monet,"
2" x 3"...**$125-$150**

Clip, fur-type, model of a seated teddy bear, black enamel,
pavé-set rhinestone face, large pearl "jelly belly," 1 1/2"
h. ....**$85-$115**

Clip, fur-type, rhinestone, spray design of pink etched glass
leaves w/turquoise, pink and lavender oval rhinestone flowers
w/blue-green enameled stems and pavé rhinestones, 1 1/2" x
2 1/4"..**$80-$100**

Clips, gold plate and art glass, art deco arrangement w/four
leaves in sunburst design, large 1 1/4" green oval glass
cabochon at the side, 2" w., 3" h., pr.
(ILLUS. p. 208)...**$135-$160**

Clip, gold-plated, fur-type, Retro-style, tapering flat metal
design w/coiled clip below large emerald cut topaz color stone,
2" ....**$50-$65**

Clip, sterling silver set w/marcasite, ornate openwork leaves in
coil design w/center cabochon-set faux aquamarine,
1 3/4"...**$75-$100**

Clip, gold-plated, Retro-style, very large center emerald-cut
topaz stone, 2" (ILLUS. p. 211). ....**$50-$75**

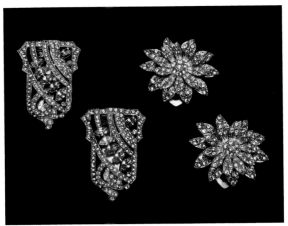

Left: Art deco dress clips, pot metal with rhinestones, c. 1925, $145; right: floral dress clips, pot metal and rhinestones, c. 1925, $165.

Retro-style clip, $50-$75.

Leo glass ornate filigree clip, $75-$100.

Shield-shaped clip, $75-$100.

Grape cluster clip, $90-$120.

Art deco-style clip, $90-$120.

Clip, rhinestone, gold ornate inverted teardrop-shaped filigree set w/large cabochon amber stones, signed "Leo Glass," 2 1/4" (ILLUS. p. 212)..**$75-$100**

Clip, rhinestone, shield shape design w/three large red cabochon marquise center stones and oval and diamond shaped red, green and blue stones, small clear stones trim, 2" x 2" (ILLUS. p. 213). ....**$75-$100**

Clip, rhinestone, art deco-style w/red cabochon stones designed as a cluster of grapes, red and clear baguettes leaves and stem, 3 1/4" h. (ILLUS. p. 214). ....**$90-$120**

Clip, rhinestone, art deco-style oval iridescent green art glass stones in inverted teardrop shape, large emerald green baguettes, trimmed w/clear square stones, 3" (ILLUS. p. 215). ....**$90-$120**

Clip, rhinestone, openwork bow design w/large oval pink, purple and aqua rhinestones, pavé-set clear stones on "ribbon," 2 1/4" x 3 1/4" (ILLUS. p. 217)............**$125-$150**

Clips, rhinestone, duette, pavé-set openwork art deco design, signed "TKF (Trifari) Clipmates," 2 5/8" (ILLUS. p. 218). ....**$175-$200**

Clips, rhinestone, duette, large amber marquise stone flowers, 3" (ILLUS. p. 219)..**$100-$125**

Rhinestone bow clip, $125-$150.

Art deco rhinestone duette clips, $175-$200.

Clip, sterling and gold-washed, large openwork flower, cluster of green glass teardrops in center, w/clear rhinestones set in tips extending from center, signed "Nettie Rosenstein," 3" x 3 1/2" (ILLUS. p. 220)..**$275-$325**

Clip, sweater-type, gold plate and pearl, chain of pearls hanging between gold-plated leaves.. **$25-$35**

Clip, sweater-type, sterling, two circles connected by 3" chain, signed "Tiffany and Co." ....**$75-$100**

Duette rhinestone clips, $100-$125.

Rosenstein flower design clip, $275-$325.

Top left and right: Bird fur clips with clear rhinestones and enameling, $125 each. Bottom: Rhodium bird brooch with clear rhinestones and enameling, $110.

EARRINGS

Earrings, art glass, red Tiffany-style iridescent large bead centers surrounded by red beads and tiny yellow bead accents, West Germany, 1 1/4"d., pr. (ILLUS. p. 223). .... **$35-$55**

Earrings, glass, hanging teardrop-style, green Peking glass, screwback-type, ca. 1925, 2 1/4" l., pr. .... **$65-$85**

Earrings, gold plate and cabochon, hoop top w/double circle drop w/blue oval cabochon set stones, drop can be removed so hoop top can be worn alone, signed "Agatha," 2" l., pr. (ILLUS. p. 224). .... **$45-$60**

Earrings, gold plate, three-dimensional flower motif w/striped gold finish, signed "Jomaz," 1 1/2" d., pr. .... **$50-$70**

Earrings, pearl, large 1/2" d. cultured pearl ball drops, clip-on type, signed "Richelieu," 1" l., pr. .... **$45-$65**

Earrings, rhinestone, drop-style, light blue top, large black pear-shaped drops w/Aurora Borealis finish, screw-on, 1 1/2", pr. (ILLUS. p. 223)... **$45-$65**

Earrings, rhinestone, slightly curved design w/horizontal rows of red baguette stones inside bordering clear round rhinestones, clip-on style, 1" l., pr. (ILLUS. p. 225)....................... **$40-$55**

Tiffany-style glass earrings, $35-$55.

Pear-shaped earrings, $45-$65.

Gold plate and cabochon earrings, $45-$60.

Red and clear rhinestone earrings, $40-$55.

Pot metal art deco earrings with clear rhinestones, $98.

Rhodium earrings with clear rhinestones, $185.

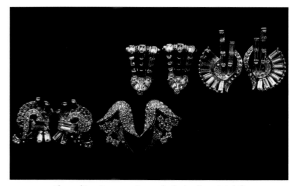

Clear rhinestone earrings, clockwise from top left:
Pennino, $85 (also has blue rhinestones); Wiesner,
$65; Jomaz floral, $56; and pot metal, $42.

Sterling earrings with clear rhinestones and faceted glass, $115.

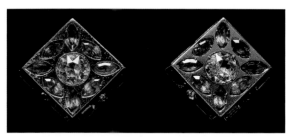

Rhodium earrings with clear and topaz rhinestones, $45.

Earring pairs, all with clear rhinestones and faux pearls, left to right: rhodium, $62; pot metal, $52; and Mazer rhodium, $75.

Earrings, silvertone fish drops, six flexible linked segments, clip-ons, signed "DKNY" Donna Karen, New York, 4" l., pr. .... **$65-$85**

Earrings, sterling silver, drop-type, openwork fish motif, screw-on, 1 3/4", pr. (ILLUS. p. 233)........................ **$60-$75**

Earrings, sterling and enamel, fan design in blue and green enamel, signed "Siam," 1 1/4" w., pr. .... **$50-$70**

Earrings, wood and plastic beads w/rhinestones, plastic coral and turquoise beads w/center orange plastic scallop shells flanking a large yellow bead, a ring of rhinestones flank shells, signed "Haskell," drop-style w/clip/screw-on mounts, 3 3/4" l., pr. (ILLUS. p. 234)... **$150-$175**

Four pairs rhodium earrings, from left: with clear and red rhinestones, $75; with clear rhinestones, $65; another with clear rhinestones, $125; with clear rhinestones and green cabochons, $65.

*Art deco earrings,
black and coral
colored glass beads, c.
1925, $175.*

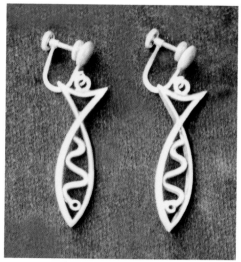

Sterling fish motif earrings, $60-$75.

Bead and rhinestone earrings, $150-$175.

Sterling earrings with clear rhinestones and red faceted glass, $295.

Assortment of earrings, from left: pot metal with clear, topaz, blue, pink, and amethyst rhinestones, $74; sterling with pink rhinestones, $125; and pot metal with blue rhinestones, $42.

Earrings with clear and open-back rhinestones, $65.

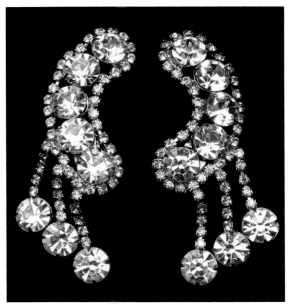

Clear rhinestone earrings, $95.

Heart earrings with pink and smoke rhinestones, $165.

Earrings, from left: Thelma Deutsch with blue rhinestones and faux pearls, $95; Kirk's Folly with clear rhinestones and faux pearls, $185; and Thelma Deutsch with clear rhinestones and faux pearls, $85.

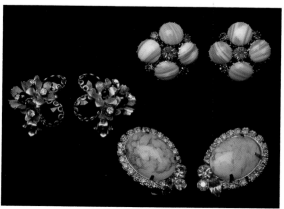

Earrings, clockwise from left: floral with black and clear rhinestones, $52; Weiss with cabochons and blue and aurora borealis rhinestones, $48; and unsigned with cabochons and topaz rhinestones, $32.

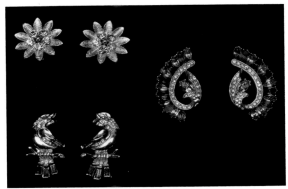

Earrings, clockwise from top left: floral with light green, pink, light blue, yellow, and lavender rhinestones, $30; with topaz, red, light blue, blue, pink, green, and clear rhinestones, $95; parrot with blue, green, and clear rhinestones, $95.

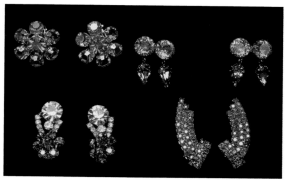

*Earrings, clockwise from top left: with orange aurora borealis
rhinestones, $18; with aurora borealis and light blue
rhinestones, $32; with red and blue aurora borealis rhinestones,
$38; and with clear and blue aurora borealis rhinestones, $48.*

Czechoslovakian earrings, brass with enameling and purple glass, c. 1925, $145.

Rhinestone earrings, c. 1950s, $70.

*Earrings with pink and blue glass, clear rhinestones
and floral design glass cabochons, c.1958, $95.*

NECKLACES

Necklace, beads, double strand composed of red, black and clear beads separated by rhinestone rondells, multi-strand drop in center, signed "Hobé," adjusts to 15" (ILLUS. p. 248). ....**$100-$125**

Necklace, beads, fringed collar-style consisting of multicolored beads, ca. 1939 (ILLUS. p. 249). ....**$170-$200**

Necklace, beads, four strands, brown, yellow, green and yellow Aurora Borealis glass beads, rhinestone baguette ends, ca. 1955, adjusts to 17" l. (ILLUS. p. 250)...............................**$70-$95**

Necklace, beads, coral glass, collar-style, hanging from gold-plated swag design chains, ca. 1955, 15" l. (ILLUS. p. 251)...**$100-$150**

Necklace, beads, double strand purple glass beads w/two very ornate overlaid beaded purple glass drops w/pink rhinestones and pink glass flowers, the center drop w/bow designs, custom made by Ian St. Gielar, 20" l. (ILLUS. p. 258)...**$1,200-$1,500**

Necklace, beaded collar-style, all-black beaded openwork designs w/triple bead drops between each design, beaded button fastener, ca. 1900, 13 1/2" l. (ILLUS. p. 259).......**$185-$220**

Hobé beaded necklace, $100-$125.

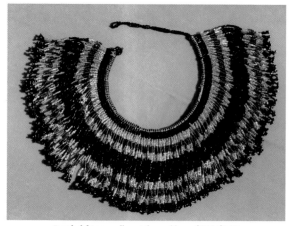

Beaded fringe collar-style necklace, $170-$200.

Aurora Borealis necklace, $70-$95.

Collar-style glass bead necklace, $100-$150.

Czechoslovakian Egyptian revival molded glass necklaces, c. 1925, from left: $155; $185; $185.

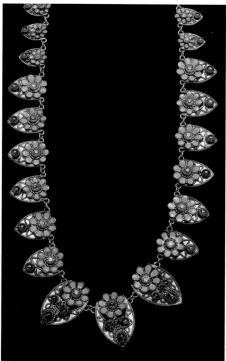

Czechoslovakian necklace, brass, enameling, topaz rhinestones, and amethyst glass, c.1925, $795.

Czechoslovakian necklace, brass, green glass, topaz glass, and pink and topaz rhinestones, c. 1925, $425.

Czechoslovakian Egyptian revival molded glass necklaces, c. 1925, from left: $225; $185.

Czechoslovakian Egyptian revival necklace, beads, and molded glass beads, c. 1925, $225.

Necklace, faceted glass beads, four graduated strands of shaded red beads w/black spacers, ornate clasp w/red and yellow beads on gold filigree, 15"-18" l. (ILLUS. p. 260). ....**$160-$185**

Necklace, carnelian and enamel, art deco-style, carved glass carnelians and enamel links w/Chinese writing, ca. 1930s (ILLUS. p. 261). ....**$100-$125**

Necklace, faux citrine and sterling silver, art deco-style, large emerald-cut faux citrine stone suspended on swag-style sterling silver chain, 15" l., stone 1 1/4" (ILLUS. p. 264)...... **$65-$85**

Necklace, glass, beads of various colors and shapes accented w/long cylindrical art glass beads, 38" l. (ILLUS. p. 265). .... **$65-$85**

Necklace, glass, bright multicolored beads w/large flat bright orange accents, 39" l. .... **$50-$65**

Necklace, green glass beads, collar-style, three rows, large gold-plated openwork metal drops, signed "Mimi di N," ca. 1960s (ILLUS. p. 266). **$185**

Necklace, gold plate, glass and pearl, multiple chains w/large 6 1/2" pendant and pink, fuchsia and moss-green rhinestones around pink/blue center cabochon, w/hanging clusters of pearl teardrops, the pearl clusters repeated along chains, signed "Florenza," about 17" l. ....**$175-$190**

*Ornate glass bead
necklace,
$1,200-$1,500.*

Early collar-style beaded necklace, $185-$220.

Art glass four-strand necklace, $160-$185.

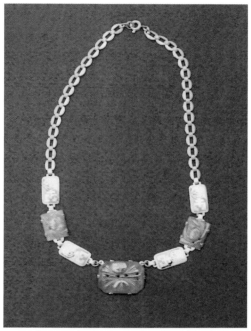

Art deco carnelian and enamel necklace, $100-$125.

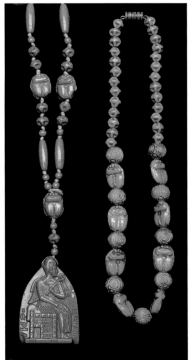

Czechoslovakian Egyptian revival molded glass necklaces, c. 1925, from left: $185; $100.

Necklace, gold plate and rhinestone, collar-style, six front panels, each made up of five horizontal rows of pink and red rhinestones, the panels separated by vertical bars of pink and red baguettes; six back panels, each w/six horizontal gold plate bars separated by vertical gold plate bars, all without rhinestones, signed "Napier," 14" adjusts to 16 1/2" (ILLUS. p. 267) ....**\$75-\$100**

Necklace, gold plate and rhinestone, three graduated chains w/large links decorated w/large gold-plated beads cabochon set w/large blue, red and green marquise rhinestones, the center chain w/large medal-lion-style star pendant, unsigned, 27" l... **\$75-\$95**

Necklace, gold-plated, red baguette rhinestone-set flower spray motif, green baguette stems on snake chains, short, signed "Corocraft" (ILLUS. p. 269). **\$125**

Necklace, gold-plated, inverted triangular links, large center faux emerald on each, purple and clear rhinestone trim, signed "Jomaz," 14 1/2" l. (ILLUS. p. 270). ....**\$250-\$300**

Necklace, gold-plated, six chains w/large four-part pink art glass stones drop, curved teardrop shapes, amber teardrop shapes, clear rhinestone trim, signed "Chr. Dior Germany," ca. 1970, 15" l w/5 1/2" l. drop, rare (ILLUS. p. 271).. **\$1,000-\$1,300**

Art deco faux citrine necklace, $65-$85.

*Multicolored
glass bead
necklace,
$65-$85.*

Mimi di N collar necklace, $185.

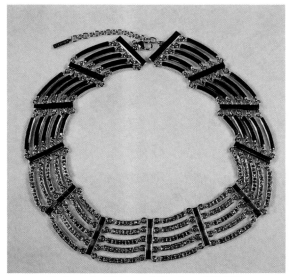

Necklace of gold plate and rhinestones, $75-$100.

Necklace, gold-plated double chain suspending seven square-shaped enameled flower motifs w/center black oval stones framed by pearls, stone and pearl accents, signed "Hobé," 15" l. (ILLUS. p. 272)..**$200-$250**

Necklace, gold-plated and rhinestone, wide filigree links alternating w/large royal blue oval and round unfoiled rhinestone flowers, large center flower on gold-plated filigree, signed "Ricarde of Hollywood," 18" l. (ILLUS. p. 273). ....**$275-$325**

Necklace, green malachite beads in graduated sizes w/green bead spacers, 23" l. ....**$85-$100**

Necklace, mosaic, rectangular red glass links w/multicolored mosaic floral design and larger floral decorated oval at center, white metal settings, 15" l. (ILLUS. p. 274)........**$125-$150**

Necklace, pale blue agate beads w/silver metal spacers, 23" l. ....**$30-$45**

Necklace, rhinestone, sterling chain set w/medium sized clear rhinestones, suspending 18 handset teardrops, signed "Coro Sterling" 14" l. (ILLUS. p. 275)............................**$125-$150**

Necklace, rhinestone, crystal and pearl, single strand of pearls alternating w/purple crystal beads suspending a 5" l. triangular pendant set w/purple cabochons and centered by two large red oval rhinestones framed by clear rhinestones, three hanging baroque pearl drops, signed "deLillo," 20" l. (ILLUS. p. 276). ....**$700-$800**

Corocraft flower spray necklace, $125.

Jomaz collar necklace, $250-$300.

Rare Dior necklace, $1,000-$1,300.

Flower motif necklace, $200-$250.

Filigree and rhinestone necklace, $275-$325.

Floral mosaic necklace, $125-$150.

Coro rhinestone silver necklace, $125-$150.

*Pearl,
crystal and
rhinestone
necklace,
$700-$800.*

*Fine Kramer
rhinestone
necklace,
$345-$365.*

Trifari rhinestone necklace, $150-$175.

Sterling silver locket necklace, $100-$125.

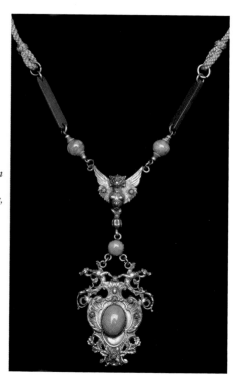

Czechoslovakian necklace, silver with green glass, c. 1930, $225.

Necklace, rhinestone, clear w/emerald-cut and pear-shaped drop and matching green round accents, signed "Kramer of N.Y.," 17" l. (ILLUS. p. 277)..................................**$345-$365**

Necklace, rhinestone and metal, square-cut aquamarine rhinestones channel-set between bars of white metal, Trifari (ILLUS. p. 278)..**$150-$175**

Necklace, sterling, pendant-type, double chain w/Egyptian profile motif on textured background, 24" l. (ILLUS. p. 279)...**$100-$150**

Necklace, sterling silver heart-shaped locket, mother-of-pearl center w/sterling military insignia, ca. 1942, w/original velvet-lined box, 19" l. (ILLUS. p. 280)..........................**$100-$125**

Necklace, sterling and amethyst, sterling chain decorated w/ center flower design of pear-shaped amethysts w/matching drop, three pear-shaped amethysts on either side, 18" l.**$140-$165**

Egyptian motif pendant and chain, $100-$150.

PENDANTS

Pendant, carnelian, heart-shaped, 1" (no chain). **$35-$50**

Pendant, enamel and white metal, cluster of red enamel cherries below antiqued white metal leaves on white metal chain w/scattered matching red glass beads, ca. 1935, 24" l. (ILLUS. p. 284)...**$75-$100**

Pendant, gold plate and rhinestone, three dimensional model of kitten w/green rhinestones eyes sitting in rope-twist circle hanging from 24" chain, 2" d. (ILLUS. p. 285)........ **$55-$75**

Pendant, gold plate, sterling and shell cameo, oval shape w/ Three Graces motif, 1 1/8" (no chain)...............**$125-$150**

Pendant, jade, pale green 2 1/4" d. pendant w/embossed Chinese characters on black cord w/slide adjuster, ca. 1925, 32" l...

Pendant, sterling, 1 1/2" pendant of 1920s style girl wearing locket, 16" l. ....**$125-$145**

Pendant, sterling and garnet, birds in nest pendant w/single garnet accent, 21" l.. **$50-$70**

Pendant, sterling, openwork 1" pendant w/heart motif and leaf and vine design, 16" l. .... **$45-$65**

Enameled cherry pendant on chain, $75-$100.

Kitten pendant in gold plate, $55-$75.

Carnegie metal and bead pendant, $195-$225.

Pendant, white metal and faux stone, pewter finish, 5" drop w/three chains set w/faux turquoise, amber, coral stones, neck chain set w/bead accents in amber, turquoise, and ivory, signed "Hattie Carnegie," chain 21" l. (ILLUS. p. 286). . **$195-$225**

Sterling silver art deco pendant with marcasites and topaz glass, $385.

Three filigree pendants, from top: with clear rhinestones, $165; with blue and clear rhinestones, $110; and with clear and blue rhinestones, $195.

PINS

Bar pin, cloisonné on copper, design of blue flowers, ca. 1920, 2 3/4" w. .... **$45-$65**

Bar pin, glass, oval shape, black, rectangular facets, Czechoslovakia, 7/8" x 1 7/8" .... **$30-$45**

Bar pin, sterling silver, iridescent blue butterfly wing under glass, oval shape, 2" w., 1/2" h. (ILLUS. p. 290) .... **$65-$90**

Bar pin, sterling silver, openwork leaves design w/center rhinestone on each leaf, 2 3/4" w., 3/8" l. (ILLUS. p.290) .... **$60-$85**

Pin, antiqued gold metal large ornate hanging chain w/an iridescent top pearl and drop and rhinestone trim, 4 3/4" l. (ILLUS. p. 291) .... **$65-$85**

Cameo pin, shell cameo carved w/a bust profile portrait of a pretty woman w/curly hair w/scroll-carved edges, set in an ornate sterling silver frame, 2" l. (ILLUS. left p. 292) .... **$175-$200**

Cameo pendant, shell cameo carved w/a seascape w/a sailing boat, set in a scalloped openwork copper frame (ILLUS. right p. 292) .... **$115-$135**

Chatelaine pin, pink gold-plated, two butterflies w/ center floral design of a pearl surrounded w/multicolored rhinestones, connected by double chain, ca. 1945 (ILLUS. top p. 293) .... **$75-$90**

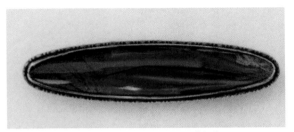

Iridescent blue butterfly bar pin, $65-$90.

Bar pin with openwork leaves, $60-$85.

Faux pearl pin, $65-$85.

Carved shell cameo pins, $175-$200 and $115-$135.

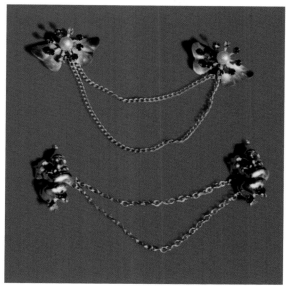

Butterfly and clown chatelaine pins, $75-$90 and $70-$85.

Chatelaine pin, white metal, two figural clowns w/red rhinestone eyes, connected by double chain (ILLUS. bottom p. 293) .... **$70-$85**

Pin, enamel iridescent flower spray, daffodil-type, light orange and yellow w/green leaves, rhinestone trim, signed "Reja," 3 1/4" h. (ILLUS. p. 295). **$145**

Pin, enamel, bow design in white enamel trimmed in gold, Trifari (ILLUS. bottom p. 296) .... **$65-$85**

Pin, enamel, model of a daisy, white enamel petals w/yellow center, unsigned (ILLUS. top p. 296) .... **$35-$50**

Pin, enamel on sterling silver, figure of Russian dancer, red jacket trimmed w/gold, white hat and blue pants and boots, ca. 1940, 2 1/4" (ILLUS. p. 297)................................**$150-$175**

Pin, enamel and rhinestone, model of a black-enameled leopard w/pavé-set rhinestone trim, Carolee Limited Edition, 1992, 3 1/4" l. (ILLUS. bottom w/tiger p. 298) .... **$100-$125**

Pin, gold plate w/black enamel and rhinestones, model of a tiger, signed "Hattie Carnegie," 3" l. (ILLUS. top p. 298) ....**$115-$135**

Pin, enamel and rhinestone, contemporary design of parrot in flight, its wings and tail of red, blue and green enamel, its body and wings trimmed w/clear pavé rhinestones, unsigned, 5" x 5 1/4"...**$125-$150**

Reja daffodil flower pin, $145.

Enameled bow and daisy pins, $65-$85 and $35-$50.

Russian dancer pin, $150-$175.

Tiger and leopard pins, $100-$125 and $115-$135.

Pin, enamel and rhinestone, dragonfly design w/black and turquoise enamel body w/blue rhinestones set in head, signed "Hattie Carnegie," 2 1/4" x 3"................................**$85-$110**

Pin, gold on sterling Retro flower spray, two large red unfoiled open set stones in flowers, 3" (ILLUS. left p. 300) **$125**

Pin, gold on sterling, two large Retro-style flowers, large turquoise rhinestone pavé-set centers, clear rhinestone trim, signed "Pennino," 2 7/8" x 2 3/8" (ILLUS. right p. 300) **$395**

Pin, gold plate and enamel, circle design w/iridescent green Christmas tree w/white enamel star attached, 1 3/8" d... **$30-$45**

Pin, gold plate, enamel and pearl, elephant w/red and green enamel saddle, a large cultured pearl on trunk, signed "Monet," 1 3/4" x 3"... **$60-$80**

Pin, gold plate and glass, large elongated trapezoid-shaped olive green glass stones arranged in flower-style, separated by citrine-colored stones, a hexagon-shaped yellow/green center stone, unsigned, 2 1/4" d..**$75-$100**

Flower spray pins, $125 and $395.

Sunburst pin with rhinestones, $125-$150.

Rhinestone, pearl and art glass pin, $150-$175.

Pin, gold plate and glass, snail design w/ribbed jade green glass body, pavé rhinestone trim, signed "Panetta," 1 1/2".. **$55-$75**

Pin, gold plate and rhinestone, Christmas tree set w/red, green, blue and clear rhinestones, 2". .... **$40-$60**

Pin, gold plate, rhinestone and enamel, bird w/long tail on branch, red, blue and green enamel feathers, two rows of tiny clear rhinestones between wing and tail feathers, green rhinestone eye, 2". .... **$40-$60**

Pin, gold plate and rhinestone, medal-style, three-dimensional sunburst design w/four pear-shaped amber stones and four smaller pear-shaped black stones radiating from large amber center stone framed by eight smaller clear rhinestones, signed "Joan Rivers," 2 1/2" d. (ILLUS. p. 301). .... **$125-$150**

Pin, gold plate and rhinestone, three-dimensional flower w/brushed gold petals and center rhinestones, in original box, signed "Coro" in block letters, ca. 1970, 2 1/4" d... **$65-$80**

Pin, gold plate, rhinestone and pearl, antiqued finish, very ornate design set w/large and small red and green rhinestones, pearls and green art glass, ornate bar w/seven chain drop in diamond-shape, unsigned Czechoslovakian, 4 1/8" h. (ILLUS. p. 302) .... **$150-$175**

Christmas lantern and tree pins, $25-$35, $40-$50, and $90-$120.

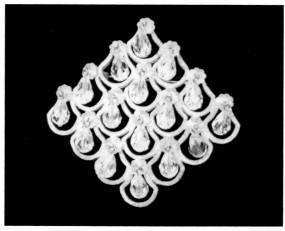

Diamond-shaped pin with crystals, $75-$100.

Ornate gold-plated pin, $65-$85.

Pin, gold plate, rhinestone, pearl and enamel, bird on branch w/iridescent blue and green enamel head and tail feathers, blue, green and red wings, the body set w/clear pavé rhinestones, green rhinestone eye, pearls and green enamel leaves on branch, signed "DJV Taiwan," 2". .... **$35-$50**

Pin, gold-plated model of a Christmas tree w/red and green iridescent enameled balls, signed "Gerys," 2" h. (ILLUS. left w/lantern and tree p. 304) .... **$25-$35**

Pin, enameled metal, model of a carriage lantern w/Christmas trim including a red enameled bow and green holly, signed "Hollycraft," 2 1/4" l. (ILLUS. top w/Christmas tree pins p. 304) .... **$40-$50**

Pin, rhinestone, model of a Christmas tree, ice blue stones on white metal, signed "Weiss," 2 1/4" h. (ILLUS. right p. 304) .... **$90-$120**

Pin, gold-plated and crystals, diamond-shaped openwork form w/rows of crystal Aurora Borealis finish hanging drops that move w/wearer, signed "Vendome," 2 1/2" (ILLUS. p. 305). .... **$75-$100**

Pin, gold-plated, antiqued, large red center stone framed by gray stones, red and gray accent stones and scrolled and leaf-form border, multichains fringe, signed "Sandor," 4" (ILLUS. p. 306). .... **$65-$85**

Gold-plated stickpin and holder pin, $60-$85.

*Ornate gold-plated pin,
$125-$150.*

Figural Scottie pin, $35-$50.

Victorian Revival design pin, $65-$95.

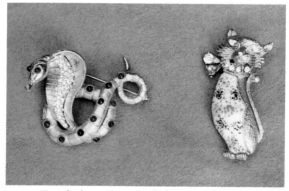

Figural cobra and cat pins, $95-$120 and $85-$115.

Rhinestone bow pin, $85-$110.

Pin, gold-plated, five "stickpin" designs in ornate holder, pearls and colored rhinestone accents, unsigned designer quality (ILLUS. p. 308).. **$60-$85**

Pin, gold-plated, ornate scrolled top w/large pear-shaped blue stone accented w/pearls and blue rhinestones, suspending five chains w/blue art glass beads and pearls, ending in center starburst medallion set w/blue art glass bead surrounded by small pearls, signed "Coro," 2 1/4" w., 5" h. (ILLUS. p. 309). ....**$125-$150**

Pin, gold-plated, model of Scottie dog, 1 3/4" w. (ILLUS. p. 310). .... **$35-$50**

Pin, gold-plated, oval Victorian Revival design, center swings around to reveal photos of two 1940s film stars, 1 5/8" x 2" (ILLUS. p. 311)... **$65-$95**

Pin, goldtone and glass, model of a standing modernistic cat w/ white glass and "coralene"-style design body, rhinestone collar and eyes, signed "Francoise" (ILLUS. right, p. 312) ....**$95-$120**

Pin, goldtone and rhinestone, model of a hooded cobra, pavé-set w/rhinestone and cabochon multicolored stones on the body and eyes (ILLUS. left w/cat pin p. 312) ....**$85-$115**

Pin, rhinestone, bow motif completely set w/large pink and clear oval stones, clear square stone trim, signed "Coro," 2 3/4" w. (ILLUS. p. 313). ....**$85-$110**

Garnet-colored rhinestone pin, $60-$85.

Floral rhinestone pin, $500-$525.

Multicolored rhinestone pin, $125-$150.

Snowflake-shaped pin, $300-$325.

Pin, rhinestone, garnet colored marquise stones set in snowflake-style design, unsigned, 1 1/2" x 2" (ILLUS. p. 315)... **$60-$85**

Pin, rhinestone, large handset Aurora Borealis stones in emerald, square and kite shapes w/large amber rhinestones in round, marquise and emerald cuts, Austria, 1 1/2" x 2 5/8"...**$75-$100**

Pin, rhinestone, large flower spray design set w/pink teardrop-shaped and emerald-cut rhinestones, large round pink stone in flower center surrounded by scalloped border set w/clear stones, stems set w/clear stones, leaves accented w/pink square-cut stones, signed "Staret," 3" x 5" (ILLUS. p. 316)..**$500-$525**

Pin, rhinestone, oval gold filigree metal set w/large topaz surrounded by green, red, blue and purple oval and marquise stones, 2 7/8" (ILLUS. p. 317). ....**$125-$150**

Pin, rhinestone and pearl, gold-plated snowflake design, large center baroque pearl w/three-dimensional layered pearl drops and clear pear-shaped and round rhinestones, signed "DeMario NY," 3" d. (ILLUS. p. 318)....................................**$300-$325**

Pin, rhinestone, gold plate and pearl, freeform granular textured design set w/turquoise stones and pearls, overlapping two large white glass teardrops, signed "Mimi di N." 2" l. .... **$70-$95**

Sterling engraved floral pin, c. 1905, $35.

Large bow design pin, $600-$700.

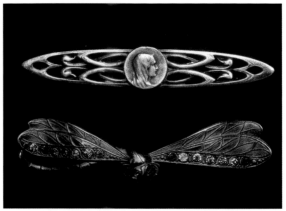

*Top: silver bar pin, c. 1900, $95; bottom: brass dragonfly
pin with green and red rhinestones, c. 1900, $130.*

Heart-shaped pin with red, green and topaz glass stones, c. 1890, $110.

Pin, rhinestone, three-dimensional gunmetal finish bow design w/very large foiled and unfoiled multi-shaped rhinestones in shades of blue, purple, green, pink and citrine, signed "Lawrence Vrba," 4" x 4 1/2" (ILLUS. p. 321).....**$600-$700**

Pin, rhinestone, cabochon-set large oval glass stones in purple, faux agates, faux pink, red and purple gemstones, signed "Robert Original," 2 1/2" x 3" ....**$165-$185**

Pin, rhinestones, grape purple border of leaves around marquise-cut and custom made leaf-shaped dark purple and pale blue stones, Aurora Borealis rhinestone centers, 2 3/4" l. ....**$75-$95**

Pin, rhinestone, model of a stork w/multicolored stones, signed "Giorgio," 2 1/2" h. **$45**

Pin, sterling silver, art deco-style figural black enamel panther, 1 3/4" (ILLUS. left p. 325) ....**$75-$100**

Pin, sterling silver, marcasite and enamel tiger on top of large black onyx circle, 2" x 2" (ILLUS. right p. 325) ..**$100-$145**

Pin, sterling silver, floral spray design, Cini ....**$325-$350**

Pin, sterling silver, Rococo flower and leaf design set w/four large crystals, Cini ....**$325-$350**

Figural panther and tiger pins, $75-$100 and $100-$145.

Fish pin, enameling with glass cabochons, c. 1930, $65.

Marcasite Christmas tree pin, $55-$75.

Circle pin with multicolored stones, $195-$225.

Figural pin with turquoise, $150-$175.

Pin in the form of a snake, $95-$120.

Reinad rhinestone orchid pin, $250-$275.

Novel wooden pin, $110-$135.

Pin, white metal, model of a Christmas tree, scalloped branches set w/marcasites and red stones, signature illegible, 2 1/8" (ILLUS. p. 327).. **$55-$75**

Pin, white metal, ornate openwork metal circle design, 1 3/8" d. raised faux topaz center, cabochon oval multicolored "agate" border, signed "Miracle," 3 1/4" d. (ILLUS. p. 328)... **$195-$225**

Pin, white metal, face of native w/hanging turquoise ball earrings, ivory plastic horn headdress w/turquoise trim, signed "Alexander Konda," 3 1/4" h. (ILLUS. p. 329)..... **$150-$175**

Pin, white metal and glass, in the form of a snake, large oval purple stones and smaller round light blue stones set as flexible body of snake, fasteners w/antique finish forming its head and tail, unsigned, 7 3/4" l. (ILLUS. p. 330)... **$95-$120**

Pin, white metal, marcasite and hematite, swirled design w/large hematite oval stone, smaller matching black rhinestones and two marcasite set swirls, West Germany, 1" x 1 1/2".. **$40-$55**

Pin, white metal and rhinestone, modeled as an orchid w/curved petals and leaves set w/gray and clear rhinestones, Reinad, 4" h. (ILLUS. p. 331)... **$250-$275**

Figural Chinese man pin, $125-$150.

Openwork pin w/purple stones, $275-$300.

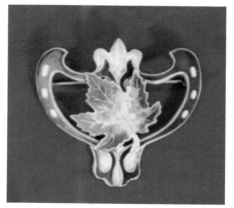

Art nouveau sash pin, $225-$250.

Pin, white metal and rhinestone, center emerald-cut purple stone in frame of clear rhinestones w/side trim of pear-shaped purple stones, clear rhinestone accents, signed "McClelland Barclay," 1 1/4" x 2 1/2"......................................**$200-$225**

Pin, white metal, rhinestone and opaline stones, floral spray set w/white opaline pear-shaped stones, trimmed w/round clear rhinestones, signed "Kramer," 2 1/2"........................ **$65-$85**

Pin, white metal and rhinestone, snowflake design set w/large emerald green marquise stones in small clear round rhinestone borders, signed "Weiss," 2 1/2" d. ....**$80-$110**

Pin, wood, carved leaf motif, three hanging celluloid chains w/brown nuts, each w/h.p. face, ca. 1935-1940 (ILLUS. p. 332). ....**$110-$135**

Pin, wood, h.p. figure of Chinese man carrying two wooden buckets on chains hanging from yoke, ca. 1935, 3" (ILLUS. p. 334). ....**$125-$150**

Pin/Pendant, rhinestone, rectangular openwork white metal setting w/assorted stones in shades of purple, alternating large pearl and glass drops in shades of purple, signed "Schreiner NY," 3" x 3 1/2" (ILLUS. p. 335)..........................**$275-$300**

Sash Pin, enamel on sterling, art nouveau-style, shaded enamel leaf motif (ILLUS. p. 336). ....**$225-$250**

RINGS

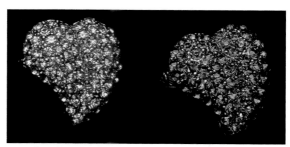

Hollycraft rings with pink and turquoise rhinestones, $84 each.

Sterling rings, from left: with marcasites,
$82, and with clear rhinestones, $84.

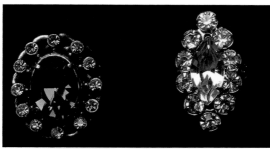

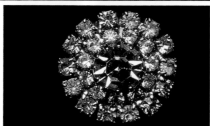

Rings, from left: Hollycraft with blue rhinestones, $110; unsigned with light blue rhinestones, $24; and unsigned with clear and light blue rhinestones, $24.

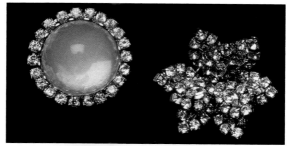

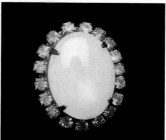

Rings, from left: with opalescent cabochon and clear rhinestones, $32; with clear rhinestones, $65; and with opalescent cabochon and clear rhinestones, $22.

Clear rhinestones rings, from left:
sterling, $65; $42; and sterling, $195.

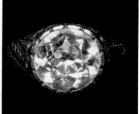

*Rings, from left: art deco with blue glass and
clear rhinestones, $155; sterling with clear
rhinestone, $195; and art deco sterling ring with
blue glass and clear rhinestones, $245.*

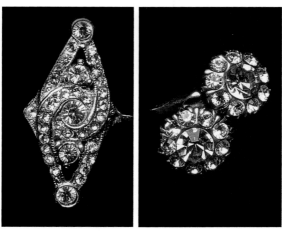

Rings, from left: sterling with clear rhinestones, $135, and gold-filled with light blue and clear rhinestones, $225.

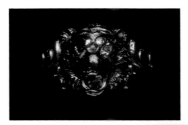

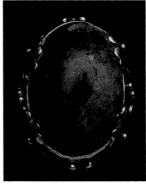

Left: 14k gold lion's head ring with rubies, c. 1900, $300; right: 14k gold ring with floral design work and green turquoise, c. 1900, $425.

Rings, c. 1950s, left: clear and light-blue rhinestones, $25; middle: blue rhinestones, $10; right: red rhinestones, $20.

A selection of rings, left to right: pot metal with clear and blue rhinestones, $85; rhodium with clear and blue rhinestones, $95; sterling with clear rhinestones and molded glass, $98; sterling with clear rhinestones, $95; and sterling with clear rhinestones, $85.

SETS

Bracelet, rhinestone, art deco, openwork links, pavé set w/ clear rhinestones, center larger red marquise rhinestones, clear emerald-cut center stones, 3/4" w. (ILLUS. p. 348, top) **$85**

Clip, rhinestone, art deco, red marquise rhinestone floral center, small clear, emerald-cut rhinestone trim, 2" (ILLUS. p. 348, top w/bracelet) **$45**

Bracelet and clip, rhinestone, art deco-style, the wide bracelet center set w/blue and clear rhinestones, together w/ matching shield-shaped clip, gold metal mount, McClelland, the set (ILLUS. p.350). ....**$575-$600**

Bracelet and earrings, metal, ornate gold metalwork links, center link set w/faux amethyst, matching pair of 1 1/2" l. drop earrings w/center-set faux amethyst, the set (ILLUS. p. 348). .... **$75-$95**

Bracelet and necklace, gold-plated, festoon-style necklace w/multi-row chains, antiqued center circular motif w/large green stone, matching 1 5/8" w. bracelet, unsigned designer quality, necklace 17 1/2" l., the set (ILLUS. p. 351). ....**$250-$275**

Art deco bracelet and dress clip, $85.

Bracelet and earrings with amethyst, $75-$95.

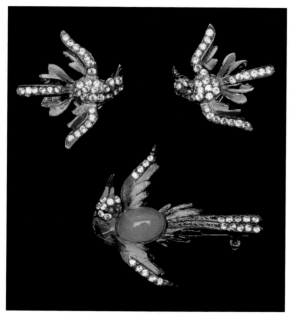

*Pot metal bird brooch and matching earrings with clear
and red rhinestones, blue cabochon, and enameling, $165.*

Art deco-style bracelet and clip, $575-$600.

Festoon-style necklace and bracelet set, $250-$275.

*Hobe necklace, bracelet, and earring set with green,
clear, citrine, and aurora borealis rhinestones, $295.*

Eisenberg rhinestone set, $565-$600.

Earrings and pin, metal and rhinestone, the pin in ornate gold metal openwork lacy circle design, together w/matching pair of 1" d. clip-on earrings, signed "Trifari," pin 1 3/4" d., the set.. **$70-$95**

Necklace, bracelet and drop earrings, rhinestone, hand-set royal blue rhinestones w/clear rhinestone trim, necklace w/central large stones and drops, the bracelet w/double row of stones and a center design, matching clip-on earrings, signed "Eisenberg," earrings 1 3/4" l., necklace adjusts to 16", the set (ILLUS. p. 353). ....**$565-$600**

Necklace and earrings, French iridescent glass, marcasite and gold plate, the 16 1/2" necklace made of nine green oval mold-formed cabochons, each w/pontil mark on back, in ornate gold-plated settings filling front half of necklace, the back half of necklace a link chain w/18 large marcasites in cup settings; the matching 2 1/8" l. drop earrings each made of two green oval cabochons in ornate settings connected by gold-plated links, the set (ILLUS. p. 355)..**$250-$275**

Necklace and earrings, gold plate and pearl, gold plate seashell design w/pearl accents in center, necklace w/14" pearl adjustable chain, screw back-type earrings, 1 1/2" l. earrings, the set (ILLUS. p. 356)... **$50-$75**

Cabochon and marcasite necklace and earring set, $250-$275.

Seashell design necklace and earrings, $50-$75.

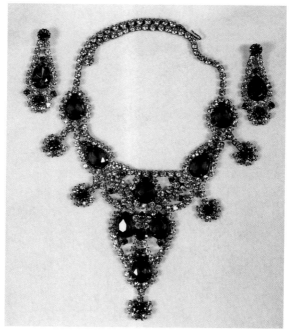

Dramatic bib-style necklace and earrings, $325-$350.

Venetian necklace and earring set, $75-$100.

Necklace and earrings, rhinestone, 16" l. necklace w/three-dimensional squares set w/clear, citrine and gray rhinestones and clear baguette centers, 5/8" each, gray rhinestone chain; matching 3/4" sq. earrings, all signed "Hobé," the set. ....**$150-$175**

Necklace and earrings, rhinestone, the 16" bib-style necklace w/eight large 3/4" royal blue crystal pear-shaped stones in descending design w/clear floral accents w/matching blue centers, all on chain made of clear rhinestones; the matching 2 1/4" l. drop earrings w/blue pear-shaped and smaller blue round stones set in frame of clear rhinestones, unsigned, the set (ILLUS. p. 357) ....**$325-$350**

Necklace and earrings, Venetian art glass, the 17" necklace made of 13 large flat red circular beads w/gold flecks and much smaller cylindrical matching spacers; simple matching 1" d. earrings, the set (ILLUS. p. 358). ....**$75-$100**

Necklace, earrings and brooch, rhinestone, the necklace composed of Aurora Borealis beads suspending a round pendant w/center-set large rhinestone surrounded by smaller stones, the 1 1/2" brooch and 3/4" d. earrings match the drop, necklace 20" l., the set (ILLUS. p. 364)............ **$300**

Chatelaine-style pin and earring set, $65-$85.

*Sterling and enamel necklace, earrings, and
brooch set, Margot de Taxco, c. 1950s, $1,500.*

Pin and earrings, rhinestone, the 3" d. pin w/large round red crystal center stone surrounded by/row of smaller red rhinestones, a third row made up of blue baguettes radiating from center w/red pear-shaped stones at ends, resembling candles; the matching 1 1/4" d. earrings w/blue center stones and alternating blue and red baguettes radiating from center, the set (ILLUS. p. 365)..**$125-$150**

Pin and earrings, rhinestone and gold plate, model of American flag set w/red, clear and blue rhinestones, matching 2" h. square screw back earrings, ca. 1955, 3/8" l. pin, the set...**$40-$65**

Pin and earrings, white metal, faux turquoise, the 5" l. chatelaine-style pin w/two chains ending in white metal blackamoor heads w/filigree trim and round turquoise stones; the matching 1" d. earrings in floral design w/turquoise stone centers, the set (ILLUS. p. 360). ....**$65-$85**

Necklace and earrings, gold-plated chain composed of circular ropetwist and rectangular textured links, some set w/green rhinestones, five drops set w/large teardrop-shaped green art glass and amber and green rhinestone accents, ropetwist frame, the center drop further decorated w/three ropetwist links set w/small green stones, together w/matching pair of 2 3/4" l. drop earrings, necklace adjusts to 17" l., the set (ILLUS. p. 363)..**$250-$300**

Necklace and earrings with green stones, $250-$300.

Aurora Borealis necklace, brooch and earrings, $300.

Red and blue pin and earring set, $125-$150.

Necklace and earrings, copper, Retro-style, 1950s, Renoir, the set (ILLUS. p. 367). ....**$115-$135**

Necklace and pins, enamel on gold, 3" l. white figural turtle on 17" chain, matching scatter pins 1 1/2" l., signed "Miriam Haskell," the set. ....**$295-$365**

Necklace and pin, rhinestone, faux cabochon sapphire links w/hand-set clear rhinestone borders, the necklace w/a single row of the sapphires and the pin w/five drops, signed "Kramer," necklace adjusts to 15", pin 3" h., the set (ILLUS. p. 369). ....**$425-$450**

Pin and earrings, gold on sterling donkey motif, large red marquise stone ears, clear baguettes mane on pin, round rhinestone tails, round rhinestones mane on earrings, signed "Corocraft," ca. 1945, pin 1 7/8", screw-on earrings 7/8", the set (ILLUS. p. 370)... **$185**

Pin and earrings, gold-plated metal, a design of openwork branches, the center w/a design of blue and gray pearls w/rhinestone trim, signed "Gasty Paris," manufactured by Grosse, dated "1969," earrings 1" w., pin 2" d., the set (ILLUS. p. 371). ....**$100-$125**

Pin and earrings, metal and glass, the pin designed as a flower w/swirled detailed gold metal petals centered w/a

Renoir copper necklace and earrings, $115-$135.

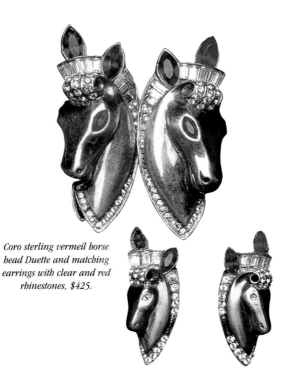

Coro sterling vermeil horse head Duette and matching earrings with clear and red rhinestones, $425.

Rhinestone necklace and pin, $425-$450.

Corocraft pin and earrings donkeys set, $185.

Gold plate and faux pearls set, $100-$125.

Amber glass pin and earring set, $120-$145.

*Top: Faux pearl bracelet with pot metal clasp and
clear rhinestones, $155. Bottom: Pot metal earrings
with clear rhinestones and faux pearls, $45.*

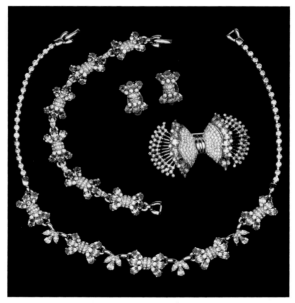

*Pennino necklace, earrings, bracelet, and brooch set with
clear rhinestones and blue open-back rhinestones, $875.*

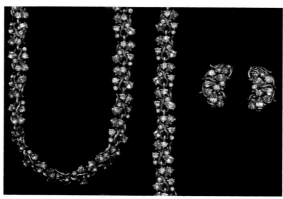

Hollycraft necklace, bracelet, and earring set with lavender, citrine, light blue, light green, blue, pink, and clear rhinestones, $300.

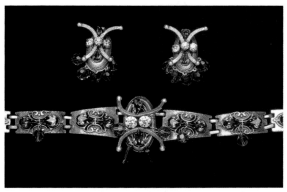

*Etruscan-style bracelet and matching earrings with
purple rhinestones and purple faceted glass beads, $265.*

large amber glass stone, together w/pair of matching earrings, unsigned, the set (ILLUS. p. 372).........................**$120-$145**

Pin and necklace, enamel on gold plate, the 2 5/8" x 3" pin w/three open iridescent purple and gold flowers w/clear rhinestone trim on petals in three-dimensional design; the 16" l. necklace w/single row of conforming flowers, chain ends, 1 1/4" w., unsigned, the set....................................**$145-$170**

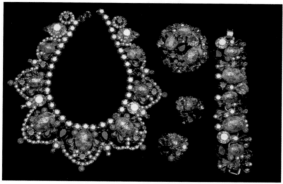

Necklace, earrings, bracelet, and matching brooch set with cabochons, green, topaz, orange, and aurora borealis rhinestones, $1,650.

*Trifari necklace, brooch, hinged bangle, and earrings
with faux pearls, green and red cabochons, blue
faceted glass, and clear rhinestones, $2,450.*

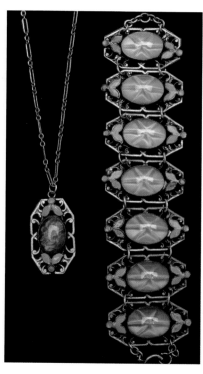

Czechoslovakian pendant and matching bracelet with green glass and enameling, c. 1920s, $395.

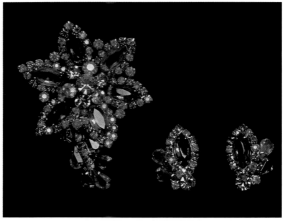

*Brooch and earring set, fuchsia and
purple rhinestones, c. 1950s, $185.*

Top: Rhodium necklace with clear rhinestones and green faceted glass, $395. Bottom: Sterling earrings with clear and green rhinestones, $85.

Clockwise from left: Pot metal and clear rhinestone clasp on faux pearl double-strand necklace, $125; pot metal and clear rhinestone clasp on triple-strand faux pearl bracelet, $65; and pot metal dress clip with clear rhinestones and faux pearls, $55.

MISCELLANEOUS

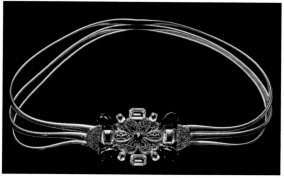

Schreiner belt with open-back clear and red rhinestones, $185.

Modern Jewelry (1920-1960s)

BRACELETS

Crystal and white gold bracelet, $764.

Bracelet, crystal and gold, art deco-style, designed w/three oval carved crystal plaques centered by diamond melée spaced by pierced and millegrained shaped 14k white gold links, 7 3/4" l. (ILLUS.). **$764**

Bracelet, diamond, art deco-style, wide design w/three repeated rectangular-shaped sections, each centrally set w/an old European-cut diamond having a total weight of approx. 2.0 cts., each section pavé-set w/round diamonds, including open, rectangular-shaped links and barrel-shaped connectors, the diamonds having a total weight of approx. 18 cts., mounted in platinum, two small stones missing, 7 3/4" l. **$16,675**

Outstanding art deco bracelet, $19,975.

Bracelet, diamond and gold, art deco-style, slender 14k filigree white gold openwork flexible mount, the center portion set w/five single and two old European-cut diamonds weighing about .65 carats, ca. 1930, 6 3/4" l. **$633**

Bracelet, diamond and platinum, centered by a spray of eight marquise and bead-set diamonds framed by straight baguettes, flanked by an openwork, graduated flexible band set throughout w/bead-set diamonds, ca. 1950, 6 1/4" l. **$3,335**

Bracelet, diamond, sapphire and platinum, art deco-style, flexible rectangular plaques set w/three marquise-cut and six triangular-cut diamonds flanked by calibré-cut sapphires, the bracelet set throughout w/transitional and single-cut diamonds, joined by hinges set w/onyx button terminals, millegrain accents, applied plaque w/store mark of Bert H. Satz, New York City, 7 1/8" l. (ILLUS.). **$19,975**

Gold and gem-set bracelet, $18,500.

Bracelet, gold (14k), Retro-style, yellow gold oval links connected by domed half links alternating w/gadrooned pink gold links, European hallmark, 8 1/4" l. **$489**

Bracelet, gold (18k yellow), Retro-style, wide fancy link design, 14k gold tongue, hallmark, 84.30 dwt. **$2,070**

Bracelet, gold, Retro-style, composed of large 14k yellow gold faceted arched rectangular flexible links, ca. 1940, 1 1/4" x 7 1/4"...**$316**

Bracelet, gold (18k bi-color) and diamond, Retro-style interlocking hexagonal links, clasp w/radiating elements, bead-set w/single-cut diamond highlights, 33.0 dwt., 7" l. **$705**

Bracelet, gold (18k), gem-set, composed of flexible circular-cut emerald, sapphire, and full-cut diamond flore, signature and hallmarks for Van Cleef and Arpels France, approx. total diamond wt. 8.64 cts., 7" l., w/original box and receipt (ILLUS.). **$18,500**

Platinum and diamond bracelet, $22,913.

Bracelet, gold (18k) and sapphire, rectangular links each w/gypsy-set oval-shaped pink sapphire, signed "RR" for Robin Rotenier, retailed by Bergdorf Goodman, 26.6 dwt., 6 3/4" l. **$2,115**

Bracelet, platinum and diamond, art deco-style composed of articulated geometric-form plaques set w/three marquise, four half-moon, 90 baguette, and 394 full and single-cut diamonds, approx. total wt. 11 cts., 7 1/4" l. (ILLUS.). **$22,913**

Bracelet, platinum and diamond, hinged, flexible geometric plaques set throughout w/ transitional-cut diamonds, spaced by plaques centered by square-cut diamonds and straight baguettes, ca. 1940, 6 1/2" l. **$18,400**

Art deco platinum and diamond bracelet, $11,163.

Bracelet, platinum, sapphire, and diamond, art deco-style, articulated links w/channel-set calibré and square step-cut sapphires and bead-set old European, rose, and single-cut diamonds, approx. total wt. 3.34 cts., 7 1/4" l. (ILLUS.). **$11,163**

Bracelet, ruby and diamond, art deco-style, designed w/five cushion-cut rubies within diamond-set links, French platinum and gold hallmarks and maker's mark, No. 57938............................ **$18,400**

Bracelet, ruby and diamond, art deco-style, flexible bracelet w/two oval links center set w/oval cabochon rubies, framed by round old European-cut diamonds and flanked by links set w/round old European-cut, baguette and square-cut diamonds and alternating w/two sections of links set w/round old European-cut diamonds bordered by a total of 48 ruby beads, ca. 1920-30, J. E. Caldwell and Co., 7" l. **$20,700**

Bracelet, sterling silver, flexibly set scrolled and shaped plaques, signed "Spratling," ca. 1940s, 7 1/4" l. **$920**

Bracelet, sterling silver, square form leaf and bead decorated links alternating w/openwork oval links centering a model of a dove, No. 14, signed "Georg Jensen," Denmark, 7" l. **$1,035**

Bracelet, sterling silver and paste, art deco-style, a floral motif w/multiple hinged plaques set w/colorless pastes, highlighted by a geometric design of green and black stones, French hallmarks, 7" l. **$1,725**

Bracelets, wood, ivory and 18k gold, hinged contemporary-style, one w/a nephrite bar, the other w/a hematite bar, signed "Amalia del Ponte," numbered "2/50" and "3/50" and dated "1967," in original felt and leather box from Sculpture to Wear, New York, pr. **$2,415**

Copper and enamel bracelet with leaf accents, c. 1950s, $145.

BROOCHES

Art deco basket-form brooch, $6,463.

Brooch, crystal and gem-set, art deco-style, flower basket shape bezel-set w/eight multi-colored stones including topaz, amethyst, beryl and kunzite cut in round, cushion and pear shapes, carved crystal basket, onyx and single- and rose-cut diamond highlights, millegrain accent, platinum mount, French platinum and gold standard guarantee stamps (ILLUS.).. **$6,463**

Brooch, diamond, art deco-style, oblong plaque-form, centering an old European-cut diamond weighing 1 ct. flanked by straight baguette-cut diamonds within an intricate frame of round and cut-cut diamonds w/a total weight of 10.80 cts.

Art deco brooch, $2,530.

for the round diamonds and 3.90 cts. for the banquettes, mounted in platinum w/an 18k white gold catch, French hallmarks.. **$6,900**

Brooch, diamond, coral and onyx, art deco-style, a brilliant-cut diamond-set open geometric design centering an oval-shaped black onyx topped w/a cabochon-cut coral w/two half-moon-shaped coral designs each accented w/a narrow band of onyx, the diamonds having a total weight of approx. 1.30 cts., mounted in platinum w/a 14k white gold pin (ILLUS.)... **$2,530**

Brooch, diamond and enamel, designed as a lily w/two pavé-set diamond leaves, polychrome guilloché enamel leaves and stem, further accented by 16 diamond stamen, 18k yellow gold, some loss to enamel, marked "Italy" (ILLUS. p. 393)... **$3,220**

Brooch, diamond and gem-set, cascade of flexibly set cabochon ruby, faceted emerald, sapphire, aquamarine and old

Diamond and enamel lily brooch, $3,220.

mine-cut diamond and champagne diamond blossoms, approx. total wt. 3.05 cts., interspersed w/engraved vines and leaves, 18k gold and platinum mount, made by Anna Bachelli.... **$14,100**

Brooch, diamond and sapphire, art deco-style, platinum oval reticulated filigree ribbon design set w/54 round old European- and single-cut diamonds and 22 square and rectangular cut sapphires, ca. 1930, 3/4" x 2". **$3,220**

Brooch, diamond and sapphire, art deco-style bow, bead-set w/72 old European and old single-cut diamonds weighing approx. 1.60 cts., edged by channel-set rectangular step-cut and calibre-cut sapphires, millegrain accents, platinum mount (ILLUS. p. 394).. **$6,463**

Diamond and sapphire bow brooch, $6,463.

Brooch, emerald, ruby and sapphire, clip-type, set w/cabochon emerald surrounded by cabochon rubies and carved sapphires, ca. 1940s, French assay and hallmark "H.L," Cartier, Paris (ILLUS. p. 395)... **$8,625**

Brooch, gem-set and enamel, calibré-cut buff-top sapphire, emerald and ruby exotic bird and flowers mounted on meandering black enamel branch within circular frame bead-set w/76 old European-cut diamonds weighing approx. 1.33 cts., platinum and gold mount, signed "E. Besson," ca. 1920s (ILLUS. p. 396)... **$16,450**

Brooch, gold (14k bicolor), aquamarine and ruby, designed as a rose and yellow gold starburst centered by a step-cut aquamarine, enhanced by six round-cut rubies................ **$546**

Brooch, gold (14k bicolor) and gemstone, designed as a butterfly w/diamond and colored gemstone accents, rose and yellow gold openwork mount, hallmarked.................... **$1,380**

Gem-set clip brooch, $8,625.

Brooch, gold (14k yellow), crown design w/seven points, each set w/a cultured pearl w/seven stickpins protruding from crown, variously set w/rose-cut diamonds, paste baroque and seed pearls, a large buff-top amethyst and a round faceted aquamarine, ca. 1950...**$460**

Brooch, gold (18k), lapis and diamond, spray of three carved lapis flowers, each centering full-cut diamond melee clusters. **$1,763**

Brooch, hardstone and enamel, Egyptian Revival design of two polychrome enamel falcon wings centered by a collet-set hardstone scarab and flanked by two serpent heads, collet-set

Gem-set and enamel bird brooch, $16,450.

diamond accents, 14k yellow gold mount, signed "Schumann Sons." **$2,070**

Brooch, hematite, crystal and marcasite, art deco-style, rectangular sterling silver and marcasite frame center set w/ quartz crystal and flanked by hematite, hallmarks for Theodor Fahrner. **$1,035**

Brooch, jade, art deco-style, the oval jade plaque in a carved and pierced foliate design w/red and green enamel and diamond terminals, 14k white gold mount (ILLUS. p. 397).. **$1,380**

Brooch, jadeite jade and diamond, art deco-style carved jade plaque bordered on both ends w/old mine-cut diamonds,

Art deco jade brooch, $1,380.

Jade and diamond brooch, $13,800.

Double clip bird brooch, $1,475.

Art deco brooch, $4,230.

weighing approx. 3.75 cts., mounted in platinum-topped 18k white gold w/14k white gold pin (ILLUS. p. 397)........ **$13,800**

Brooch, mixed metal, modeled as a water lily w/beaded center and leaves, chased and engraved 18k yellow gold, hammered silver leaves and lily pads, signed "Janiyé." **$345**

Brooch, platinum and diamond, double clip-type, designed as two birds w/long curled tail feathers, encrusted w/single-cut diamonds, perched on a baguette diamond branch, red stone eyes, ca. 1940s (ILLUS. p. 398)......................................**$1,475**

Brooch, platinum, diamond and onyx, bow-shaped art deco-style, bead-set w/110 old European and single-cut diamonds,

Art deco double clip brooch, $6,325.

channel-set French-cut onyx and millegrain accents, pierced gallery (ILLUS. p. 399). **$4,230**

Brooch, quartz and 14k yellow gold, handcrafted large nugget-textured mount set w/a large quartz crystal rough set w/a blue/gray Baroque cultured pearl, marked "NKT.BRUYN," 2" w., 3 1/4" l. **$431**

Brooch, ruby and diamond, art deco-style w/a center sugar loaf cabochon-cut ruby within a finely worked open frame decorated w/rose-cut diamonds, each end w/an old European-cut diamond, all within a border of small old European- and old mine-cut diamonds, two diamonds missing, mounted in platinum and 18k yellow gold. **$10,120**

Brooch, ruby and diamond, art deco-style, double clip-type, designed w/eight oval cabochon rubies and set throughout w/bead-set circular-cut diamonds, 12 baguette diamond accents, platinum mount (ILLUS. p. 401). **$6,325**

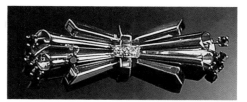

Retro bicolor sapphire brooch, $1,725.

Brooch, sapphire and diamond, floral bouquet design set w/21 round faceted blue sapphires and 18 round brilliant-cut diamonds, the stems set w/35 straight baguette diamonds, tied by a white gold knot set w/nine single-cut diamonds, platinum mount, ca. 1950, 1 1/4" x 2".. **$4,600**

Brooch, sapphire and gold, Retro-style stylized 14k yellow and rose gold bow centered by three bead-set diamonds mounted in platinum, circular and calibré-cut sapphire terminals, inscription on back (ILLUS.)... **$1,725**

Brooch, sapphire, ruby and diamond, art deco-style, double clip-type, set w/marquise shield, round and baguette diamonds, 10 carved oval cabochon sapphires and eight cabochon rubies, platinum and 18k gold mount (ILLUS. p. 402)... **$4,600**

Art deco double clip brooch, $4,600.

Brooch, silver glazed earthenware and fused glass, abstract design in shades of green and blue glaze, ceramic backing, abstract silver mount, impressed on reverse "Elsa" for Elsa Freund, ca. 1960. .... **$1,093**

Brooch, turquoise, pearl and gold, insect form, w/14k yellow gold legs and wings, turquoise body, pearl head and garnet eyes, ca. 1930 (ILLUS. p. 404) **$280**

Brooch clips, diamond, a scrolled ribbon and floral motif, each clip centering a transitional old European- to round brilliant-cut diamond weighing approx. 3.75 cts., the leaves, scrolls and borders decorated w/124 round diamonds having a total weight of approx. 7 cts., mounted in platinum w/18k white

Diamond brooch clips, $25,300.

gold clip backs and brooch attachment, brooch attachment w/maker's mark, ca. 1930, Rome, pr. (ILLUS.). **$25,300**

Brooch/pendant, gold (14k yellow), diamond and ruby, Retro-style, a domed circle bead-set w/six round rubies in a star motif w/a ribbon design at center highlighted by seven round diamonds, pendant loop, 22.9 dwt. **$690**

Clip brooch, diamond, ruby and platinum, Retro-style, pavé-set and circular-cut diamond-set caps surmounted by a similarly set swag, suspending a spray of 18 square-cut rubies and eight tapered baguette-cut ribbons, Austrian import assay marks, hallmark. **$4,715**

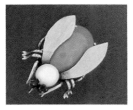

Gold and turquoise insect brooch, $280.

Clip brooches, emerald, sapphire, ruby and diamond, art deco "tutti frutti"-style, two-part rectangular form set in the center w/carved emeralds, sapphires, rubies and baguette-cut diamonds within a double row of round diamonds, diamonds total weight 2.2 cts., mounted in platinum w/18k white gold clip backs and brooch attachment, pr. **$6,900**

Clip brooch, gold (14k) and diamond, Retro-style, rectangular form arranged w/contrasting rose and yellow gold in a stepped pattern, surmounted by circular and baguette-cut diamonds, signed "Cartier." **$2,645**

CLIPS

Art deco flower basket clip, $4,313.

Clip, diamond, emerald, ruby and sapphire, art deco-style, designed as a flower basket encrusted w/circular and baguette diamonds, cabochon sapphire, carved emerald and ruby highlights, platinum mount (ILLUS.). **$4,313**

Clip, diamond and platinum, stylized "S" form, the platinum mount set w/14 round brilliant-cut diamonds weighing about 4.90 carats, six emerald-cut diamonds weighing about 4 carats, two pear-shaped and four marquise-cut diamonds weighing about 2.90 carats, ca. 1960, 1 1/2" x 2".......................... **$5,750**

Clips, diamond and platinum, art deco-style, designed as chevrons centering a large round-cut diamond and enchanced

Diamond art deco dress clip, $3,408.

w/numerous round brilliant-cut and emerald-cut diamonds, approx. 8.00 cts., pr... **$21,850**

Clips, dress-type, diamond and platinum, art deco-style, two detachable triangular clips set throughout w/35 baguettes, two kite-shape and 174 single- and full-cut diamonds, w/convertible white metal frame attachment, pr. (ILLUS. of one)....... **$3,408**

Clip, dress-type, pink diamond and ruby dress clip, art deco design, centered w/emerald-cut pink diamond weighing 1.90 cts. framed by square step-cut rubies, further enhanced by bead-set single-cut diamonds and two diamond baguettes weighing approx. 2.26 cts., square step-cut ruby accents, platinum mount, ca. 1930 (ILLUS. p. 407)... **$35,250**

Pink diamond and ruby dress clip, $35,250.

Ruby and diamond dress clips, $5,875.

Art deco sapphire and diamond dress clips, $3,173.

Clips, dress-type, platinum, ruby and diamond, five prong-set circular-cut rubies and 61 full-cut and baguette diamonds, approx. total wt. 4.48 cts., w/14k gold brooch attachment (ILLUS. p. 408)..**$5,875**

Clips, dress-type, sapphire and diamond, art deco-style, bead-set w/72 full and single-cut diamonds, channel-set, square, step and calibre-cut highlights, millegrain accents, platinum mount, w/brooch conversion, pr. (ILLUS.). **$3,173**

Clip, gold (18k yellow), ruby and diamond, modeled as a stylized Christmas tree, the base set w/11 graduated old mine- and old European-cut diamonds, the body composed of circular swirls set w/42 round faceted rubies, ca. 1950, 1 1/2" w., 3" h. **$1,495**

EARRINGS

Gold and emerald earrings, $1,456.

Earpendants, platinum, ruby and diamond, chandelier designed as cascade of flexibly set circular-cut rubies and full, marquise and pear-cut diamonds, platinum mount, signed "HW" for Harry Winston, pendants detachable. **$11,750**

Earrings, emerald, diamond and gold,14k yellow gold leaf scroll forms centered w/two emerald-cut emeralds and three small round diamonds, ca. 1940, pr. (ILLUS.). **$1,456**

Earrings, emerald, diamond and platinum, designed w/bezel-set circular old mine-cut diamond tops, suspending diamond-set trefoils and similarly styled caps terminating in tumbled pear-shaped emerald beads, ca. 1920s, missing end finials on terminals, in original S.J. Phillips fitted box, pr.......... **$16,100**

Earrings, gold (18k yellow), designed as dogwood blossoms, center w/gold bead decoration, French clip-back, Tiffany and Co., together w/original box, pr...**$978**

Earrings, gold (14k bi-color) and gem-set earrings, designed as a cluster of yellow and rose gold blossoms, full-cut diamond and garnet accents, 7.4 dwt., pr. **$558**

Earrings, jade and diamond, art deco-style, a large carved mottled green and white jadeite jade disk accented w/rose-cut diamonds in scrolled designs, suspended from round and rose-cut diamonds, mounted in platinum and 18k yellow gold, jade has some hairline cracks, ca. 1926, w/maker's mark, w/leather box, pr. **$5,060**

Earrings, pearl, large pear-shaped natural pearl drops, each topped w/a round brilliant-cut diamond attached to a button-shaped pearl ear pad surrounded by round diamonds, can be worn independently without the detachable drops,

Sapphire and diamond earring, $2,875.

mounted in 14k white gold, ca. 1930, w/original leather box and EGL report stating the pearls are saltwater natural pearls, pr. **$57,500**

Earrings, sapphire and diamond, designed as a stylized bowknot, centered by an oval faceted sapphire w/channel-set sapphire and bead-set diamond highlights, 18k white gold, ca. 1940s, signed "Kutchinsky," pr. (ILLUS. of one, p. 411) **$2,875**

Top: sterling vermeil earrings, clear rhinestones and amethyst glass, c. 1940, $125; bottom left: sterling vermeil floral design earrings, rhinestones, c. 1940, $110; bottom right: Mazer sterling vermeil earrings, green glass and clear rhinestones, c. 1940, $155.

LAVALIERES

Lavaliere, platinum, diamond and sapphire, art deco-style w/a cushion-cut sapphire within an openwork, geometric mount set throughout w/old European-cut diamonds, millegrain accents, suspended by a delicate trace-link chain, signed "Tiffany and Co.," 16 1/4" l. (ILLUS.). **$4,370**

Art deco-style lavaliere, $4,370.

LOCKETS

Locket, gold (14k), diamond and enamel, art deco-style, centered exotic bird in flight w/bead-set single-cut diamond body and ruby eye, black enamel background w/delicate white enamel border, opening to reveal two interior compartments, platinum bail. **$2,350**

NECKLACES

Carnelian and enamel necklace, $4,700.

Necklace, aquamarine and platinum, art deco-style large teardrop-shaped aquamarine pendant suspended from a platinum-topped 14k gold floral engraved box and rectangular link chain, hallmark for Allsopp and Allsopp, 15 1/2" l. **$3,738**

Necklace, carnelian and enamel, art deco design, five graduating floral carved and pierced carnelian plaques joined by bow-form celadon green and black enamel links, seed pearl accents, 14k gold mount, partially obliterated hallmark for "Carter Howe and Gough," 16 1/2" l. (ILLUS.) **$4,700**

Necklace, diamond and ruby, art deco-style featuring a slightly graduating row of square-cut calibré rubies and round brilliant-cut diamonds, 18k white gold mounting, approx. diamond wt. 3.00 cts.. **$2,185**

Necklace, emerald and diamond, art deco-style, a large pendant in the Oriental flower vase motif designed from carved Columbian emeralds and round diamonds, w/black enamel and cabochon-cut emerald accents, joined by a black enamel loop to a similarly designed emerald, diamond and black enamel chain, mounted in platinum, numbered, w/ French hallmarks and maker's mark, ca. 1925, Mauboussin, Paris. **$167,500**

Necklace, gold (18k yellow) and diamond, designed w/an open circle and oval drop w/prong-set diamonds suspended from a pavé-set terminal, completed by a double barrel link chain w/collet-set diamonds, approx. total diamond wt. 2.40 cts., obliterated signature for Cartier, ca. 1950s............. **$4,025**

Necklace, gold (18k) and diamond, open abstract-form links, each bezel-set w/full-cut diamonds, signed "C. Deneuve"

for Catherine Deneuve, approx. total wt. 0.82 cts.,
15" l. **$1,410**

Necklace, sterling silver, abstract open form links, designed by
Henning Koppel, hallmark for Georg Jensen, ca. 1947,
15 1/2" l.. **$1,150**

Necklace, sterling silver, quartz and marcasite, art deco-
style, designed w/marcasite-set hinged silver links centered
by an abstract knot terminating in a faceted fancy shape
smoky quartz, green stone accents, hallmarks for Theodor
Fahrner. **$6,900**

PENDANTS

Art deco diamond and sapphire pendant, $4,830.

Pendant, diamond and sapphire, art deco-style, elongated flared design composed of four movable sections decorated w/round diamonds w/baguette-cut, triangular-shaped and calibré-cut sapphires set in geometric designs, attached to a fine link chain w/rectangular-shaped, barrel clasp decorated w/two small diamonds, two triangular-shaped and two baguette-cut sapphires, platinum mounting and chain, approximately 21 1/2" l. (ILLUS.) **$4,830**

Emerald and diamond pendant, $9,200.

Pendant, emerald and diamond, art deco-style, a collet-set old mine-cut diamond suspending a cut-corner square-cut emerald set in 18k yellow gold within a quatrefoil frame of bead-set old mine-cut diamonds, platinum mount, surface nicks to emerald, completed by a rectangular trace link platinum chain, 17" l. (ILLUS.) **$9,200**

Pendant, enamel and onyx, art deco-style, navette-shaped silver, ivory and black enamel plaque centered by a sugarloaf onyx, marcasite highlights, suspended from a black cord, French hallmarks, signed "Batik." **$805**

*Egyptian Revival beetle
pendant, $18,800.*

Pendant, gold, enamel and Favrile glass, Egyptian Revival
beetle pendant, centered by a blue Favrile glass beetle set
within a rectangular plaque decorated w/dark blue-green
enamel corners, signed "Tiffany and Co., no. 379," also
stamped "Gold and Other Metals," ca. 1920, minor chips to
enamel (ILLUS.). **$18,800**

Pendant, jade and gold (18k yellow), foliate carved jade
plaque, surmounted by a gold scrolled cap, topped by a tumbled
oval pink tourmaline, beaded gold bail (ILLUS.
p. 420). **$2,070**

Carved jade pendant,
$2,070.

Pendant, sapphire and gold, Retro-style, the 14k yellow gold bow edged w/a row of prong-set oval light blue, violet and golden sapphires, suspending a ruby-set accent spray, pin stem from brooch removed, signed "KS" (ILLUS. p. 421)...... **$1,380**

Pendant, sterling silver and amethyst, designed w/graduated concentric circles, intersected by a sterling bar w/a cabochon amethyst terminal, No. 143, signed "Georg Jensen." **$1,495**

Gold and sapphire spray pendant, $1,380.

Pendant, silver and enamel, art deco-style, square plaque w/clipped corners surmounted by an urn and flower design on a green and black enamel ground, hallmark for David. **$1,725**

Pendant, tourmaline and diamond, art deco-style, centering a pinkish-purple tourmaline carved in a three-dimensional floral design w/a small diamond pistil, in a frame of old mine-cut (one replaced w/an old European-cut) and baguette-cut diamonds mounted in platinum and 18k white gold (ILLUS. p. 422). **$9,200**

Art deco tourmaline and diamond pendant, $9,200.

Pendant and chain, gold and semi-precious stone, egg-form, tested 18k yellow gold mount set w/eight oval cabochon multicolored and lace agate stones each measuring 9 1/2mm x 13 mm, together w/an 18k yellow gold rope chain, ca.1950, 20" l...**$230**

Pendant/brooch, citrine, pearl, coral and gold, art nouveau-style, the 18k yellow gold delicate scrolling leaf mount set w/a large heart-shaped scotch-colored citrine weighing about 50 carats flanked by two leaping silver panthers, the top set w/four freshwater pearls, the bottom suspending a yellow gold, orange coral and baroque pearl tassel, ca. 1960, 2" x 4"...**$1,265**

Pendant/brooch, diamond, art deco-style, the elongated hexagonal shape set w/old mine-cut diamonds, pierced platinum-topped 14k white gold mount w/millegrain accents, one diamond missing, hallmarked F.N. **$1,495**

Pendant/brooch, platinum and diamond, art deco-style, oblong openwork form bead-set w/57 old European and full-cut diamonds, total wt. 2.20 cts., detachable bail. **$2,468**

Pendant/brooch, platinum, diamond and emerald, art deco-style, openwork plaque set w/23 old European- and single-cut diamonds and 18 emerald and green stone accents, millegrain accents, deployant bail. **$2,938**

Cameo pendant/brooch, shell, art deco-style, 14k yellow gold scalloped latticework decorated pentagonal mount set w/a large cameo depicting a seated classical woman w/a young child within a garden landscape, ca. 1930, 3" x 3 1/4". **$316**

Pendant-locket, platinum, diamond and faux green jade enamel, art deco-style oval locket w/millegrain platinum mount set w/three circular-cut diamonds, faux green jade "en plein" enamel surface. **$920**

Pendant-necklace, diamond and platinum, art deco-style, detachable pendant centering a flexibly set faceted pear-shaped yellow diamond weighing approx. 9 cts., frame, bail and necklace further bezel and bead-set w/one marquise and 164

*Art deco diamond and platinum
pendant, $193,000.*

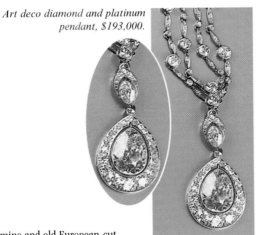

old mine and old European-cut
diamonds weighing approx. 5.25
cts., millegrain accents, platinum
mount, 16" l. (ILLUS.).. **$193,000**

Pendant-necklace, sterling silver, marcasite and glass
baguettes, art deco-style, pierced rectangular pendant set
w/carved blue and pink flowerheads over a row of clear glass
baguettes, set throughout w/marcasites, completed by a baton-
sur-link chain, one marcasite missing, chain not silver,
32" l. **$489**

Sterling pendant with quartz, maker's mark unreadable, c. 1955, $450.

PINS

Platinum, sapphire and diamond bar pin, $3,055.

Bar pin, diamond, black onyx and platinum, art deco-style, the narrow rectangular platinum mount w/a central shield-form openwork design set w/two old mine-cut diamonds each weighing about .75 and .60 carats alternating w/four rectangular and one calibré-cut onyx stones, flanking the central design are 14 square scissor-cut black onyx stones, ca. 1930, 3" l. **$1,840**

Bar pin, platinum and diamond, art deco-style, central diamond-shaped motif set w/an old mine-cut diamond, surrounded by 54 graduated old mine- and rose-cut diamonds, ca. 1920-30, 3 1/4" l. **$2,185**

Bar pin, platinum, sapphire and diamond, art deco bezel, bead-set throughout w/66 old European, French, baguette and single-cut diamonds, approx. total wt. 1.98 cts., rectangular and

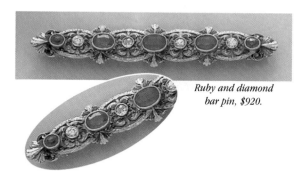

Ruby and diamond bar pin, $920.

triangular-cut sapphire accents, millegrain accents and pierced
gallery (ILLUS. p. 426). **$3,055**

Bar pin, ruby and diamond, yellow gold and silver scrolled
openwork design alternately set w/five rubies and four round
diamonds (ILLUS.). **$920**

Bar pin, sapphire and diamond, art deco-style, long
narrow form set in the center w/three old European-cut
diamonds, accented w/four French baguette-cut sapphires
w/diamond-set flower heads, flanked by 12 French baguette-cut
sapphires, mounted in platinum w/a 14k yellow gold pin, ca.
1930s. **$4,485**

Art deco sapphire and diamond pin, $4,700.

Pin, coral, onyx and diamond, art deco-style geometric buckle design of coral w/onyx and diamond highlights, platinum mount.. **$2,990**

Pin, jadeite and enamel, art deco-style, black, green and yellow enamel pagoda framing a pierced jadeite plaque depicting a bird among flowers, 14k gold mount, hallmark for Sloan and Co.. **$3,055**

Pin, moonstone, sapphire and platinum, art deco-style, centered by a sugarloaf moonstone, flanked by square-cut sapphires, edged w/rectangular moonstones, all channel-set, oval

Amethyst heart-shaped pin, $862.

moonstone terminals, wiretwist filigree accents, yellow gold pin stem, signed "Tiffany and Co.," 3" l............................. **$24,150**

Pin, onyx, diamond and ruby, art deco-style, onyx circular plaque w/round diamond and calibré-cut ruby terminals, platinum mount, minor chip to onyx, signed "J.E. and Co." for J.E. Caldwell and Co., No. K-5045.................................... **$9,775**

Pin, ruby and diamond, designed as a circular band of channel-set rubies and single-cut diamonds surmounted by a diamond floret, platinum and millegrain mount.......................... **$2,760**

Pin, sapphire and diamond, art deco-style, bezel-set w/one faceted oval and two cushion-cut sapphires, w/46 old European and old mine-cut diamonds, approx. total wt. 1.88 cts.,

*Diamond and sapphire pin/
pendant, $1,840.*

millegrain accents, platinum mount, French hallmark and
guarantee stamps (ILLUS. p. 428) **$4,700**

Pin/pendant, amethyst and diamond, heart-shaped
amethyst surrounded by 20 prong-set round diamonds, 14k
yellow gold mount (ILLUS. p. 429)....................................**$862**

Emerald and diamond stickpin, $1,495.

Pin/pendant, diamond and sapphire, center set round diamond w/rose-cut diamonds in the circular white gold openwork design and framed by 12 round sapphires (ILLUS. p. 430). **$1,840**

Stickpin, emerald and diamond, art deco-style, cushion-cut emerald in a pierced and platinum millegrain mount edged w/12 old mine-cut diamonds (ILLUS.). **$1,495**

Stickpin, enamel, designed as a beagle head, diamond eye, 14k yellow gold engraving and chasing, hallmark. **$575**

RINGS

Art deco diamond ring,
$17,625.

Ring, diamond, art deco-style, twin stone design, set w/two old European-cut diamonds, separated by baguettes in stepped geometric design, platinum mount. **$23,000**

Ring, diamond, art deco-style, box-set w/three old European-cut diamonds, gallery and shoulders pierced in a scroll design, platinum mount, size 6. .... **$8,338**

Ring, diamond, art deco-style, set w/three old European-cut diamonds, approx. total wt. .60 cts., within a pierced and engraved platinum mount set w/four single-cut diamonds, millegrain accents, size 6 3/4... **$881**

Ring, diamond, art deco-style, transitional-cut solitaire diamond weighing approx. .94 cts. framed by 12 circular-cut diamonds, shoulders set w/six circular-cut diamonds, millegrain accents, incised shank, size 5 1/4.................................... **$2,350**

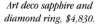
Art deco sapphire and diamond ring, $4,830.

Ring, diamond, art deco-style, set w/a pear-shaped solitaire diamond weighing approx. 2.35 cts. further set w/six straight baguettes, nine single- and six transitional-cut diamonds, platinum mount signed "Shreve and Co., no. B9550," size 8 (ILLUS. p. 432)... **$17,625**

Ring, diamond, 14k yellow gold and platinum-topped oval mount set w/three round old European-cut diamonds framed by 20 old mine-, old European- and single-cut diamonds, ca. 1910, Edwardian. **$1,035**

Ring, diamond, yellow radiant-cut solitaire diamond weighing 1.64 cts., framed by 10 faceted half-moon-shaped diamonds weighing 2.13 cts., shoulders pavé-set w/20 full-cut diamond melée weighing 0.31 cts., custom-made 18k white gold mount, size 7 1/2 .... **$9,106**

Art deco sapphire and diamond ring, $10,063.

Ring, diamond solitaire, gentleman's, Retro-style, 18k white gold box illusion mount set w/one old mine-cut diamond. **$2,760**

Ring, diamond solitaire, gentleman's, Retro-style centering a round old European-cut diamond, 14k yellow gold mount, ca. 1940. .... **$4,830**

Ring, diamond and gold, art deco dinner-type, tested 18k white gold filigree mount set w/11 round old European-cut diamonds weighing about 1 carat, ca. 1930, size 6 3/4. .... **$690**

Ring, diamond and gold, art deco-style, 14k white gold filigree mount w/one marquise diamond, ca. 1920. .... **$11,200**

Art deco sapphire and diamond ring, $3,055.

Ring, diamond and onyx, art deco-style, navette-shaped onyx tablet bezel-set w/old European-cut diamond weighing approx. 2.89 cts., platinum and 18k gold mount, size 1 1/2 (evidence of solder). **$6,169**

Ring, diamond and platinum, art deco-style, bezel-set cushion-shaped old mine-cut diamond weighing approx. .81 cts., framed by 18 old mine-cut diamonds, platinum openwork mount w/ millegrain accents, size 5 3/4... **$1,528**

Ring, diamond and platinum, two-stone, the platinum four-prong mount set w/two square-cut diamonds each weighing about 1.75 carats flanked by four straight baguette diamonds weighing about .40 carats, ca. 1940, size 6 1/2.............. **$8,050**

Ring, emerald and diamond, art deco-style, 18k yellow gold silver washed crown holding center oval cabochon emerald surrounded by two rows of round diamonds flanked on each side by round diamonds, ca. 1930. .... **$896**

Sapphire and diamond ring, $4,406.

Ring, gold (14k white) and diamond, art deco-style, set w/one round old European-cut diamond approx. 1.05 cts., flanked by two smaller old mine- and European-cut diamonds, approx. .40 cts., ca. 1930.. **$1,495**

Ring, gold (18k), diamond and platinum, Retro-style, two old European-cut and six single-cut diamonds vertically set in platinum tiered shoulders, size 6 ....**$294**

Ring, opal and garnet, art deco-style, centered by an oval opal framed w/28 channel-set demantoid garnets, 18k white gold mount w/diamond shoulders, French hallmarks. **$2,185**

Ring, platinum and diamond, art deco-style, dinner-type, platinum braided design mount centered by a bezel-set round old European-cut diamond surrounded by 34 round old mine- and old European-cut diamonds, ca. 1930. .... **$2,415**

Ring, platinum and diamond, centered w/European-cut diamond weighing approx. 1.19 cts., w/single-cut diamond high-lights, millegrain accents, pierced gallery, size 6 1/2. .... **$2,585**

Ring, sapphire and diamond, art deco-style, openwork pierced platinum mount w/millegrain accents centered by a collet-set circular-cut sapphire, framed by eight old mine-cut diamonds, size 6 1/2. ....**$863**

Ring, sapphire and diamond, centrally designed w/two rows of faceted calibé-cut sapphires w/a row of round brilliant-cut diamonds forming a border on each side, having an approx. total diamond weight of 0.50 ct., mounted in platinum, numbered and signed "Cartier," ca. 1930. ....**$6,325**

Ring, sapphire and diamond, art deco-style w/center prong-set cushion-shaped sapphire surrounded by 13 old European-cut diamonds, platinum mount, 14k white gold shank (ILLUS. p. 433). **$4,830**

Ring, sapphire and diamond, art deco-style, centered by a sugarloaf sapphire surrounded by 76 old mine-cut diamonds and 16 French-cut sapphires, platinum mount (ILLUS. p. 434). **$10,063**

Ring, sapphire, diamond and platinum, art deco-style, a cabochon sapphire measuring approx. 12.7 x 10.71 x 7.95 mm, the millegrain accented openwork shoulders set w/old mine- and single-cut diamonds, approx. total weight .80 cts., platinum mount, size 5 3/4 (ILLUS. p. 435)...................................**$3,055**

Ring, sapphire, diamond and platinum, prong-set w/cushion-cut sapphire weighing 3.01 cts. flanked by old mine-cut diamonds, approx. total diamond wt. 1 ct., open gallery, size 5 (ILLUS. p. 436).. **$4,406**

Ring, sapphire, diamond and platinum, art deco-style, centering a prong-set cushion-cut sapphire weighing 3.07 cts., flanked by diamond trillions, approx. total weight 1.20 cts., shoulders accented by 16 circular-cut diamonds and incised foliate designs, millegrain accents, pierced gallery, platinum mount, signed by Tiffany and Co., size 7 (ILLUS.)...... **$25,850**

Ring, white gold (18k), sapphire and diamond, bezel-set w/ sapphire cabochon flanked by swirls of pavé-set diamonds interspersed w/shaped lilac chalcedony plaques, approx. 12.48 x 9.65 x 5.90 mm, size 6, French hallmarks, marked "Van Cleef and Arpels, NY63876."... **$5,581**

Extraordinary art deco Tiffany ring, $25,850.

SETS

Bracelet and brooch, gold (18k yellow), art deco-style, flexible belt design w/three rectangular and oval interlocking links, together w/matching brooch converted from one of the bracelet links, ca. 1930, bracelet 6" l., the set. **$1,380**

Brooch and earrings, citrine and diamond, the brooch designed as a four-leaf clover w/heart-shaped citrine leaves centered by a circular-cut diamond w/a bead-set diamond stem, 14k yellow gold mount, matching earrings, the set..**$546**

Brooch and earrings, jade, moonstone and diamond, art deco-style, a double-clip brooch (one moonstone missing) and matching pair of clip earrings, platinum mounts, signed "Seaman Schepps," the set... **$8,338**

Necklace and bracelet, gold (18 k), "Connections" necklace and bracelet designed as interlocking circles, signed "Paloma Picasso and Tiffany and Co.," w/original suede sleeve, necklace 16 1/2" l., bracelet 7 1/2" l., the set................ **$2,233**

Necklace and earrings, garnet and seed pearl, the necklace set w/faceted garnet clusters, the center three accented by seed pearls, together w/a matching pair of clip earrings, gilt silver mounts, ca. 1950s, hallmark, the necklace 14" l., the set.. **$1,035**

Necklace and earrings, sterling silver, the necklace of hinged rectangular plaques decorated w/an applied foliate design, together w/matching earrings, signed "USA Georg Jensen Inc.," earrings No. 419B, necklace No. 429B, the set. **$633**

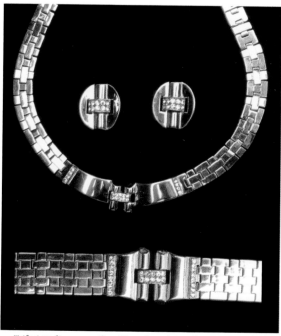

Trifari sterling vermeil necklace, bracelet, and earring set, clear rhinestones, c. 1940s, $475.

MISCELLANEOUS

Cameo cuff buttons and shirt studs, hardstone, the cuff buttons and three shirt studs depicting the profile of a classical female, 14k yellow gold mount, stamped "S.L. and Co." for Savage, Lyman and Co., Montreal, w/original fitted box. **$805**

Lorgnette, diamond and crystal, art deco-style, the reverse intaglio depicting a dancer within a diamond and frosted crystal frame, diamond-set bail, completed by a platinum and collet-set diamond chain, 28" l. (ILLUS. p. 443)............ **$8,625**

Lorgnette, diamond and platinum, art deco-style, filigree platinum openwork mount set w/28 round old European-cut diamonds, a hinged release opens to hinged eyeglasses, together w/a platinum chain set w/eight round old European-cut diamonds, ca. 1920, 19 1/2" l.. **$2,875**

Watch fob, hardstone, Egyptian Revival-style, suspending a faience scarab and two engraved 14k yellow gold frames, hardstone cylinder seals, solder evident. **$978**

Diamond and crystal lorgnette, $8,625.

Art Plastic Jewelry

BRACELETS

Bracelet, bangle-type, Bakelite, alternating sections of Bakelite and brass, 3 1/4" (ILLUS. p. 445). **$175**

Bracelet, Bakelite, bangle-type, carnelian orange, w/carved leaves and flowers, 5/8" w. **$80-100**

Bracelet, Bakelite, bangle-type, chartreuse green/yellow marbled, no carving, 1/2" w. **$35-50**

Bracelet, Bakelite, bangle-type, yellow, no carving, 7/8" w. **$55-75**

Bracelet, Bakelite "School Days" charm-type, the links designed as rulers suspending seven plastic, Bakelite or felt school-related charms. **$345**

Bracelet, Bakelite and faux pearl, cuff-style, hinged design w/an abstract foliate motif of carved green Bakelite set w/faux golden pearls. **$2,185**

Bracelet, Lucite, bangle-type, double row of applied black cone-shaped designs around entire bracelet, ca. 1965, 2" w. **$40-60**

Bakelite and brass bangle bracelet, $175.

Raised dot Bakelite bangles with rhinestones, from left: marbled green and orange, marbled tobacco brown and butterscotch, dark marbled blue green with light green, $600 each.

Celluloid bracelet with Bakelite charms, $225.

Left: Celluloid and rhinestone bangle, $265;
right: celluloid and rhinestone bangle, $195.

Carved Bakelite bangles, left: black, $600; right: butterscotch, $500.

Bakelite bangle, $950.

BROOCHES

Leaf brooch, moonglow with rhinestones, $110.

Patriotic anchor brooch, red Bakelite and plastic, $495.

Flower brooch with thermoset plastic, $38.

*Top-carved and reverse-carved and painted
applejuice Bakelite and black Bakelite brooch, $550.*

Left: Sterling vermeil fish brooch with carved Lucite belly, $495; right: sterling vermeil rabbit brooch with Lucite belly and clear and red rhinestones, $295.

Horse brooch with Lucite body, $950.

Celluloid brooch with rhinestones, $125.

*Rooster brooch, celluloid with red, green,
pink, aurora borealis rhinestones, $88.*

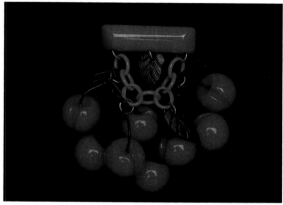

Brooch with carved Bakelite cherries, c. 1935-1945, $750.

CLIPS

Carved Bakelite leaf clips, $85-$110.

Clips, Bakelite, marbleized butterscotch yellow circles, densely carved leaves, 1 3/4" d., pr. (ILLUS.).................... **$85-$110**

Clip, dress, Bakelite, art deco-design in green marbleized w/dark blue, graduated cylinders w/chrome circles on sides, 2 1/4" h. (ILLUS. p. 461)... **$95-$125**

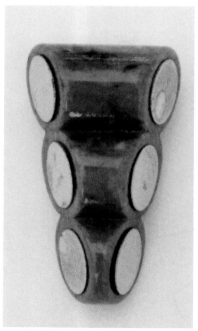

Art deco-design Bakelite dress clip, $95-$125.

Floral dress clips, butterscotch Bakelite, $125 for the pair.

EARRINGS

Red Bakelite heart earrings, $225.

Thermoplastic earrings with rhinestones, from top: $80, $85.

Plastic earrings, $35.

NECKLACES

Chain necklace with flower drops, $50-$65.

Necklace, gold-plated chain suspending six lacy green plastic flowers w/gold metal bead center, ca. 1935, 14" l. (ILLUS.) ....**$50-$65**

Necklace, plastic and rhinestone, amber-colored beads marbled to look genuine, set w/black rhinestones, black faceted glass spacers, 12" adjusts to 15" ....**$35-$50**

Brass necklace with green Bakelite leaf charms, $325.

*Faceted red
Bakelite
necklace,
$98.*

PENDANTS

Bakelite pendant and chain with rhinestones, $375.

Cameo pendant on chain, celluloid and Bakelite, $195.

PINS

Carved Bakelite pin, $175.

Pin, Bakelite, carved palm fronds and coconuts resembling acorns, dark green, ca. 1930s, 3 1/4" l. (ILLUS.). **$175**

Pin, Bakelite, figural articulated design, black body and arms, brown legs, painted face, red topknot, holding a white stick and orange shield, ca. 1930...**$805**

Pin, gold plate, enamel and plastic, large and small white daisies w/raised yellow plastic centers, green leaf, signed "Weiss," 2 3/4" h..**$50-$75**

RINGS

*Top left: Bakelite ring, $95; top right: marbled green and butterscotch
Bakelite ring, $145; bottom: marbled green Bakelite ring, $95.*

Laminated Lucite rings, $20 each.

SETS

Necklace and earring set, molded plastic, $95.

*Thermoplastic hinged bangle and earring
set with blue rhinestones, $185.*

Watches

Lapel watch, enamel and diamond, enameled portrait surrounded by rose-cut diamond scrollwork and green guilloché enamel, verso depicting a lute and doves, 18k yellow gold case, white porcelain dial w/black Arabic numerals, dust cover inscribed "Grand Prix/Paris/1889," suspended from a fleur-de-lis pin set w/old European-cut diamonds, seed pearl accents, 18k yellow gold mount, one small diamond missing, minor enamel loss, boxed.. **$2,875**

Lapel watch, enameled cherries motif, hanging from brown bar pin, larger cherry contains watch by Clifford **$125**

Lapel watch, gold-filled (12k yellow), floral spray pin w/watch set as a flower, signed "CA" pierced by an arrow (Carl-Art), 2 3/8" h. .... **$150-$200**

Lapel watch, gold-plated, snake motif w/green cabochon eyes and top of head, pavé clear rhinestones head, watch is inside coil of snake's body, original tag Kenneth Jay Lane, signed "La Tour" 17 jewels, body is also signed K.J.L., 3 1/2" w. (ILLUS. p. 480) .... **$250-$300**

Lapel watch, gold-plated, Retro-style horse head motif, watch w/works visible on reverse, signed "Monocraft" (old Monet mark), 2 1/4" (ILLUS. p. 481) ....**$150-$175**

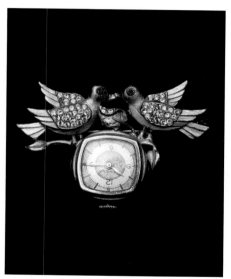

Geneva watch brooch with enameling
and clear and green rhinestones, $395.

Man playing guitar watch pin, Gotham, enameling, c. 1940, $345.

Lapel watch, gold plate and rhinestone, figural ship's wheel set w/baguettes on the spokes, suspended on a chain from a rhinestone-set bow design, sweep seconds hand, signed "Pierce," 2" l. (ILLUS. p. 482) ....**$145-$170**

Lapel watch, sterling silver and marcasite, floral spray design w/watch set as flower, second hand, signed "Merit," 3" (ILLUS. p. 483) ....**$265-$295**

Pendant watch, diamond and sapphire, round case encrusted w/bead-set round diamonds set in platinum and sapphires set in 18k yellow gold, diamond-set bow, movement No. 16622, porcelain dial w/black Roman numerals, scroll hands, ca. 1905, Tiffany and Co., Edwardian, accompanied by Tiffany and Co. appraisal. **$8,050**

Pendant watch, diamond and sapphire, art deco-style, diamond and sapphire encrusted case centered by a bezel-set marquise diamond, bail set w/a pear-shaped and round diamond, mounted in platinum w/millegrain accents, platinum bar link and seed pearl chain, No. 30735, Tiffany and Co., 19" l. **$5,463**

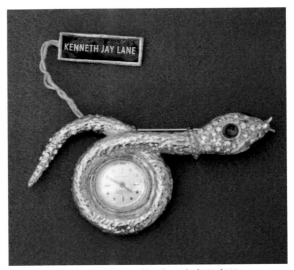

Gold-plated snake motif lapel watch, $250-$300.

Horse head form lapel watch, $150-$175.

Figural ship's wheel lapel watch, $145-$170.

Floral spray lapel watch, $265-$295.

Brooches, clockwise from top left: rotary floral with watch, clear and blue rhinestones, $385; Harvel fish with watch, clear rhinestones, green cabochons and enameling, $395; woman with watch and clear, blue, red, and green rhinestones as well as enameling, $345; and Pierce floral with watch, clear rhinestones, faux pearls, and enameling, $465.

Glossary

A

Algrette: Jewels mounted in a shape resembling feathers or a feather motif.

A-jour Setting: An open work setting in which the bottom portion of the stone can be seen. Also a setting in which the metal has open work.

Albert Chain: A watch chain for a man or a woman with a bar at one end and a swivel to hold a watch at the other.

Alma Chain: A chain with broad ribbed links.

B

Baguette: A stone cut in the shape of a narrow rectangle.

Banded Agate: Agate that has bands of lighter and darker colors. It can be onyx (black/white), cornelian (orangish red/white), or sardonyx (brown/white).

Bangle: A rigid bracelet often tubular and hinged.

Basse-taille: An enameling technique in which a translucent enameling is applied to an engraved metal surface.

Baton: A stone cut in the shape of a long narrow rectangle.

Beauty Pins: Pins popular from the mid-1800s until after the turn of the 20th century. Usually under two inches long with rounded ends.

Belcher Mounting: A claw-type ring mounting on which there were many variations. Popular from the 1870s through the 1920s.

Benoition Chain: A chain worn suspended from the top of the head that encircled the head and dropped down onto the bosom.

Bezel: A metal rim that holds the stone in a ring, a cameo in its mounting, or a crystal on a watch.

Black Amber: A misnomer for jet.

Bloomed Gold: A textured finish on gold that is created by immersing in acid to give it a matte pitted effect.

Bog Oak: Wood preserved in the bogs of Ireland and used to make jewelry during the Victorian era.

Bohemian Garnet: A dark red pyrope garnet.

Brilliant Cut: A cut that returns the greatest amount of white light to the eye. It usually has 57 or 58 facets. Usually used for diamonds or other transparent stones.

Briolettes: A teardrop-shaped cut covered with facets.

Brooch: An ornamental piece of jewelry that has a pin back for affixing it to clothing or hats. Usually larger in scale than the ones referred to as "pins."

Brooch-watch: A watch with a brooch affixed so it is worn as one would wear a brooch.

Bulla: A round ornamental motif found in ancient jewelry.

C

Cabochon: A stone cut in round or oval shape in which the top is convex shaped (not faceted).

Cairngorm: Yellow brown to smoky yellow quartz named after the mountain range in which it is found in Scotland.

Calibre Cut: Small stones cut in the shape of squares, rectangles, or oblongs used to embellish jewelry.

Cameo: A layered stone in which a design is engraved on the top layer and the remainder is carved away to reveal the next layer, leaving the design in relief. Also done in shell, coral, and lava.

Cameo Habille: A type of cameo in which the carved head is adorned with a necklace, earrings, or head ornament set with small stones.

Cannetille: A type of metal decoration named after the type of embroidery made with fine twisted gold or silver thread. It is done using thin wires to make a filigree pattern. Used frequently in England in 1840.

Carat: A unit of weight for gemstones. Since 1913 one metric carat is one-fifth of a gram or 200 milligrams.

Carbuncle: Today used to refer to a garnet cut in cabochon. In the middle ages it referred to any cabochon-cut red stone.

Cartouche: An ornamental tablet used in decoration or to be engraved, usually symmetrical.

Celluloid: One of the first plastics. A compound of camphor and gun cotton. Highly flammable.

Champlive: An enameling technique in which enamel is put into areas engraved or carved into the metal.

Channel Setting: A type of setting in which stones of the same size are held in place by a continuous strip of metal at the top and bottom, literally creating a channel for the stones.

Chasing: The technique of embellishing metal by hand using hammers and punches to make indentations, thus raising the design.

Chatelaine: A metal clasp or hook worn at the waist from which hang a variety of useful items suspended by chains.

Chaton: The central or main ornament of a ring.

Cipher: A monogram of letters intertwined.

Claw Setting: A style of ring setting in which the stone is held by a series of vertically projecting prongs.

Clip: A piece of jewelry resembling a brooch but instead of having a pin stem to fasten into clothing, it has a hinged clip that hooks over and into the fabric. Very popular from the 1920s-1940s. Sometimes made as a brooch that incorporated a double clip. It could be worn as a brooch or disassembled and used as a pair of clips.

Cloisonné: An enameling technique in which the enamel is placed into little preformed compartments or cells built on to the metal.

Collet Setting: A ring setting in which the stone is held by a circular band of metal.

Coronet Setting: A round claw setting in crown-like design.

Cravat Pin: The same as a tie pin.

Creole Earrings: A hoop style in which the metal is thicker and wider at the bottom than at the top.

Croix a la Jeanette: A piece in the form of a heart from which a cross is suspended. A form of French peasant jewelry. Circa 1835.

Crossover: A style of ring, bracelet or brooch in which the stoneset decorative portions overlap and lie alongside each other.

Crown Setting: An open setting resembling a crown.

Cultured Pearl: A type of pearl induced and stimulated by man to grow inside a mollusk.

Curb Chain: A chain in which the oval flattened links are twisted so that they lie flat.

Cushion Cut: A square or rectangular shape with rounded corners. Also called "antique cut."

Cut Steel Jewelry: Jewelry made of steel studs which are faceted. Popular from the 1760s until the late 19th century.

Cymric: A trade name used by Liberty & Co. for articles sold by them which were designed and manufactured by English firms. The name was adopted in 1899.

D

Designer: A person who designs jewelry. Occasionally they were also makers of jewelry.

Damascene: The art of encrusting metals with other metals.

Demi-parure: A matching set of jewelry consisting of only a few pieces such as a necklace with matching earrings or a bracelet with matching brooch.

Demi-hunter: A watch with a lid over the face in which there is a circular hole in the middle to expose the hands of the watch.

Dog Collar: A type of necklace consisting of rows of beads or a wide band worn snugly around the neck.

Doublet: An assembled stone consisting of two materials, usually garnet and glass.

E

Edwardian Jewelry: Jewelry made during the reign of Edward VII, 1901-1910, that does not fall into the art nouveau or Arts & Crafts movement category.

Electro-plating: The process of covering metal with a coating of another metal by using electrical current.

Electrum: A pale yellow alloy made by mixing 20% gold and 80% silver.

Enamel: A glass-like material used in powder or flux form and fired onto metal.

Engine-turning: Decoration with engraved lines produced on a special lathe.

Engraving: A technique by which a design is put into a metal surface using incised lines.

Eternity Ring: A ring with stones set all the way around. Symbolizing the "never-ending" circle of eternity.

F

Fede Ring: An engagement ring which features two hands "clasped in troth."

Ferronniere: A chain that encircles the forehead as portrayed in Leonardo da Vince's "La Bel Torronnier." A 16th century adornment; it was revived during the Victorian era.

Filigree: Ornamental designs made by using plain twisted or plaited wire.

Fob: A decorative ornament suspended by a chain usually worn with a watch.

Foil: A thick layer or coating used on the back of stones to improve their color and brilliance.

French Jet: It is neither French nor jet, instead, this term usually refers to black glass.

G

Gate: A channel in a mold through which the molten metal flows during the white metal spin-casting process. Also refers to that part of the cast piece that is wasted.

Gilloche: Engraved decoration of geometric design achieved by engine turning. Usually used as a base for translucent enamel.

Girandole: Brooch or earring style in which three pendant stones hang from a large central stone.

Gunmetal: An alloy of 90% copper and 10% tin that was very popular in the 1890s.

Gutta-percha: A hard rubber material made from the sap of a Malayan tree. Discovered in the 1840s, it was used for making jewelry, statuary, and even furniture.

Gypsy Setting: A type of setting in which the stone is set down flush in the mounting.

H

Hairwork Jewelry: Jewelry made using hair worked on a table or jewelry that incorporates hair and was worked on a palette.

Hallmark: A group of markings used on silver or gold in England since 1300 to designate the fineness of the metal, the town in which it was assayed, and the name of the maker.

Holbeinesque: A style of jewelry popular in England in the 1870s. Its inspiration was from the design of Hans Holbein the Younger.

Hunting Case: A watch that has a lid covering the face. A case spring is activated by pushing on the crown causing the lid to pop open.

I

Incise: A line cut or engraved in a material.

Intaglio: A design cut below the surface of stone. The opposite of a cameo.

Intarsia: The use of stones to make a picture by cutting them out and inlaying them flushed into a background stone.

J

Jabot Pin: A type of stick pin worn on the front of ladies' blouses.

Jet: A very lightweight black or brownish black material that is a variety of the coal family.

K

Karat: Pure gold is 24 karats. The karat of gold alloy is determined by the percentage of pure gold. For instance 18K gold is 750 parts pure gold and 250 parts other metal or 18 parts pure gold and 6 parts other metal.

L

Lava Jewelry: Jewelry made of the lava from Mt. Vesuvius. Usually carved into cameos or intaglios and sold as souvenirs of the "grand tour."

Laveliere: A light scaled necklace usually consisting of a pendant or pendants suspended from a chain. In the 1890-1910 era it usually had a baroque pearl appendage. The word is probably derived from the Duchess de la Valliere, a mistress of Louis XIV.

Line Bracelet: A flexible bracelet composed of stones of one size or graduating in size, set in a single line.

Luckenbooth Brooches: So called because they were sold in street stalls (Luckenbooths) near St. Giles Kirk in Edinburg. The motif usually consisted of one or two hearts occasionally surrounded by a crown. When the motif included the initial "M," the brooch was referred to as a Queen Mary brooch.

M

Macle: A flat-bottomed diamond crystal.

Mandrel: A replica made of wax or white metal used as a core onto which metal is deposited during the electroplating process.

Marcasite: A misnomer that is now the commonly accepted trade name for pyrite. Popular from the 18th century onwards.

Marquise: A boat-shaped cut used for diamonds and other gem stones. Also called a "navette" shape.

Memento Mori: "Remember you must die." Grim motifs such as coffins, skeletons, etc. Worn as a reminder of one's mortality.

Millegrain: A setting in which the metal holding the stone is composed of tiny grains or beads.

Mizpah Ring: A popular ring of the 19th century consisting of a band with the word Mizpah engraved across the top. "May the Lord watch between me and thee while we are absent from the other."

Mosaic: A piece of jewelry in which the pattern is formed by the inlaying of various colored stones or glass. Two types of mosaic work are Roman and Florentine.

Mourning Jewelry: Jewelry worn "in memory of" by friends and relatives of the deceased. Often sums of money were set aside in one's will to have pieces made to be distributed to mourners attending the funeral.

Muff Chain: A long chain worn around the neck and passed through the muff to keep it secure.

N

Necklace Lengths: Choker-15 inches, Princess-18 inches, Matinee-22 inches, Opera-30 inches, Rope-60 inches long.

Nickel Silver: A combination of copper, nickel, zinc, and sometimes small amounts of tin, lead, or other metals.

Niello: A decorative technique in which the metal is scooped out (in the same manner as champlive) and the recessed area is filled with a mixture of metallic blue black finish. The technique dates back to the Bronze Age.

O

Old Mine Cut: An old style of cutting a diamond in which the girdle outline is squarish, the crown is high and the table is small. It has 32 crown facets plus a table, and 24 pavilion facets plus a culet.

P

Paste Jewelry: Jewelry that is set with imitation glass gems. Very popular in the 18th century, it provides us with many good examples of the jewelry from that time period.

Parure: A complete matching set of jewelry usually consisting of a necklace, earrings, brooch, and bracelet.

Pate de Verre: An ancient process in which glass is ground to powder, colored, placed in a mold, and fired. It was revived in the 19th century and used to make many pieces of art nouveau jewelry.

Pavé Setting: A style of setting in which the stones are set as close together as possible, presenting a cobblestone effect.

Pebble Jewelry: Scottish jewelry (usually silver) set with stones native to Scotland. Very popular during the Victorian era.

Pendeloque: A faceted drop-shaped stone (similar to a briolette) that has a table.

Pietre dure: (Hard Stone). Flat slices of chalcedony, agate, jasper, and lapis lazuli used in Florentine mosaic jewelry.

Pinchbeck: An alloy of copper and zinc invented by Christopher Pinchbeck in the 1720s that looked like gold. It was used for making jewelry, watches, and accessories. This term is very misused today. Some dealers refer to any piece that is not gold as "pinchbeck."

Pique: A technique of decorating tortoiseshell by inlaying it with pieces of gold and silver. Popular from the mid-17th century until Edwardian time.

Platinum: A rare heavy, silvery white metallic element that is alloyed with other metals and used to make fine pieces of jewelry.

Plique-a-jour: An enameling technique that produces a "stained glass effect" because the enamel is held in a metal frame without any backing. An ancient technique, it was revived and used extensively by art nouveau designers.

Poincon: A French term for the mark on French silver similar to the English hallmark.

Posy Ring: A finger ring with an engraved motto (often rhymed) on the inner side.

R

Regard Ring: A finger ring set with six stones of which the first letter is each spell REGARD. The stones most commonly used were: Ruby, Emerald, Garnet, Amethyst, Ruby and Diamond.

Repoussé Work: A decorative technique of raising a pattern on metal by beating, punching, or hammering from the reverse side. Often called embossing.

Rhinestone: Originally rock crystal found along the banks of the Rhine River. Today, a misnomer for colorless glass used in costume jewelry.

Rhodium: A white metallic element that is part of the platinum group. Because of its hard reflective finish it is often used as a plating for jewelry.

Riviere: A style of necklace containing individually set stones of the same size or graduating in size that are set in a row without any other ornamentation.

Rose Cut: A cutting style in which there are 24 triangular facets meeting at the top with a point. The base is always flat. Diamonds cut this way are usually cut from macles.

Ruolz: A gilded or silvered metal named after the French chemist who invented the process.

S

Sautoir: A long neck chain that extended beyond a woman's waist. Usually terminating in a pendant or tassel.

Signet Bangle: A hinged tubular bracelet with a central plaque for engraving. Very popular in the 1890-1910 time period.

Signet Ring: A ring with a central plaque on which one's initials were engraved. Sometimes a seal or crest was used.

Scarf Pin: A straight pin approximately 2 1/2 inches long with a decorative head. It was used between 1880-1915 to hold the ties in place. It is the same as a tie pin.

Seed Pearl: A small pearl weighing less than 1/4 grain.

Shank: The circle of metal that attaches to the head of a ring and encircles the finger.

Sprue: A rod attached to the base of a mold model to provide a channel in the mold through which the wax can flow. This sprue also becomes a part of the wax and consequently a part of the casting.

Star Setting: A popular setting in the 1890s in which the stone is placed in an engraved star and secured by a small grain of metal at the base of each point.

Stomacher: A large triangular piece of jewelry worn on the bodice and extending below the waistline. An 18th century style that was revived during the Edwardian period.

Swivel: A fitting used to attach a watch to a chain. It has an elongated spring opening for attaching the watch. The swivel allows the watch to hang properly.

Synthetic: A manmade material with the same physical, chemical, and optical properties as the natural. Not to be confused with imitation.

T

Taillé d'Epergne: An enameling technique in which engraved depressions are filled with opaque enamel.

Tiffany Setting: A round six-prong mounting with a flare from the base to the top.

Trademark: The mark registered with the U.S. Patent Office that identifies a wholesaler or retailer.

V

Vermeil: Gilded silver. Sterling silver with a gold plating.

W

White Gold: An alloy of gold, nickel, and zinc developed in 1912 to imitate the popular platinum.

White Metal: A base metal of tin, lead, bismuth, antimony, and cadmium used in the manufacturing of costume jewelry. The tin content can vary from 17 to 92 percent. It can be electroplated to any color desired.

Index